Focus on the

WONDER YEARS

Challenges Facing
the American Middle School

Jaana Juvonen
Vi-Nhuan Le
Tessa Kaganoff
Catherine Augustine
Louay Constant

Prepared for the
Edna McConnell Clark Foundation

RAND EDUCATION

The research described in this report was conducted by RAND Education for Edna McConnell Clark Foundation.

ISBN: 0-8330-3390-5

The RAND Corporation is a nonprofit research organization providing objective analysis and effective solutions that address the challenges facing the public and private sectors around the world. RAND's publications do not necessarily reflect the opinions of its research clients and sponsors.

RAND® is a registered trademark.

Cover design by Barbara Angell Caslon

Published 2004 by the RAND Corporation
1700 Main Street, P.O. Box 2138, Santa Monica, CA 90407-2138
1200 South Hayes Street, Arlington, VA 22202-5050
201 North Craig Street, Suite 202, Pittsburgh, PA 15213-1516
RAND URL: http://www.rand.org/
To order RAND documents or to obtain additional information, contact
Distribution Services: Telephone: (310) 451-7002;
Fax: (310) 451-6915; Email: order@rand.org

Preface

Today in the United States there are nearly 9 million students in public middle schools (typically, schools that include grades 6 through 8). Middle school youth are especially vulnerable to multiple risks. For example, the process of social alienation that ultimately leads students to drop out of high school often starts during the middle grades. Hence, the middle school years are critical in setting the trajectories for subsequent life success.

How well are middle schools serving our young? The RAND Corporation set out to assess the state of American middle schools and identify the schools' major challenges. The research team collected and synthesized literature that describes pertinent research conducted during the last 20 years. We reviewed the issues that have received substantial attention, as well as those that have not been recognized or discussed. We supplemented the literature review with our own analyses of some of the most recent national and international data.

This monograph describes our findings. To assess the *effectiveness* of middle *schools*, we focus heavily on middle school *students* and student outcomes, such as academic achievement. But we also review research on the other key players, including teachers, principals, and parents. We provide context for our analyses by describing the historical changes that have shaped today's middle schools and the key organizational and instructional practices and multicomponent reforms that U.S. middle schools have adopted in recent years. Finally, we summarize the main challenges identified and discuss future directions for middle-grade education.

This work should be of interest to a wide audience of those who are concerned about and responsible for young teens, including education policymakers and administrators at the national, state, district, and local levels; private advocacy and philanthropic organizations; teachers; parents; and researchers. The monograph is not the "how-to" guide that we all might wish for. Rather, our goal is to provide a broad context for future decisionmaking. We hope that our review and analyses provoke new ways of thinking and help point the way for those who must address the many challenges facing America's middle schools.

This research was carried out under the auspices of RAND Education. Any opinions, findings, conclusions, or recommendations are those of the authors and do not necessarily reflect the views of the Edna McConnell Clark Foundation, which funded this project.

The RAND Corporation Quality Assurance Process

Peer review is an integral part of all RAND research projects. Prior to publication, this document, as with all documents in the RAND monograph series, was subject to a quality assurance process to ensure that the research meets several standards, including the following: The problem is well formulated; the research approach is well designed and well executed; the data and assumptions are sound; the findings are useful and advance knowledge; the implications and recommendations follow logically from the findings and are explained thoroughly; the documentation is accurate, understandable, cogent, and temperate in tone; the research demonstrates understanding of related previous studies; and the research is relevant, objective, independent, and balanced. Peer review is conducted by research professionals who were not members of the project team.

RAND routinely reviews and refines its quality assurance process and also conducts periodic external and internal reviews of the quality of its body of work. For additional details regarding the RAND quality assurance process, visit http://www.rand.org/standards/.

Contents

Figures

Tables

Summary

During the middle school years, young teens undergo multiple physical, social-emotional, and intellectual changes that shape who they are and how they function as adults. The schools young teens attend play a critical role in shaping these futures. Therefore, the state of the U.S. middle school is—or should be—of concern to all of us. Unfortunately, the reputation of U.S. middle schools today leaves in doubt whether these schools serve teens well. Middle schools have been called the Bermuda Triangle of education and have been blamed for increases in behavior problems, teen alienation, disengagement from school, and low achievement.

RAND undertook a comprehensive assessment of the American middle school to separate the rhetoric from the reality. The passage of the federal No Child Left Behind Act of 2001 (NCLB), with its emphasis on test-based accountability and sanctions for failing schools, makes such an assessment particularly timely and important.

This monograph describes our findings. The focus is on U.S. public middle schools—schools that serve as an intermediary phase between elementary school and high school, typically consisting of grades 6 through 8. The monograph is designed to

- identify the challenges middle schools face today
- describe and evaluate the effectiveness of current efforts to improve middle schools
- highlight the many areas lacking rigorous research
- suggest new ways of thinking about the middle school and its functions
- help prioritize the challenges and make recommendations when possible.

The research team reviewed 20 years of relevant literature and analyzed existing national and international data. We focused on eight areas:

- the historical context for middle schools
- the evidence supporting some key instructional and organizational practices
- academic achievement of middle school students
- conditions known to affect students and their academic performance

- qualifications of middle school teachers
- challenges principals face
- declining parental involvement
- middle school reform efforts.

In each chapter, we review the latest research evidence to identify the major challenges middle schools are facing and make general recommendations when appropriate. We also explore ideas stemming from the broader field of education and highlight the areas in which additional research might yield new solutions.

Findings

Lessons from History

Our historical review shows that many of today's concerns about young teens and the proper way to educate them are similar to the concerns that have been expressed for the past 100 years. The issues and the solutions that were endorsed at any particular time, including the concept of an intermediate school between elementary and high school, often had more to do with labor market needs or the capacity of school buildings than with educational or developmental considerations. There has also been an ongoing debate about the proper role of the middle school, with tensions between

- the need for middle schools to ease the transition from elementary school, with an emphasis on the developmental needs of young teens, versus the need to facilitate the transition to high school, with an emphasis on academic rigor
- the need to increase educational attainment by providing schooling for all, versus the need to improve college preparation for high-achieving youth.

Research suggests that the onset of puberty is an especially poor reason for beginning a new phase of schooling, inasmuch as multiple simultaneous changes (for example, the onset of puberty and school transfer) are stressful for young adolescents and sometimes have long-lasting negative effects. Furthermore, the few studies that compared schools with different grade configurations suggest that young teens do better in K–8 schools than in schools with configurations that require a transition to an intermediary school. Recent studies also suggest that students do better in schools that both foster personal support and emphasize academic rigor.

Core Middle School Practices

Middle school education has long been criticized as being unresponsive to adolescents' developmental needs. Interdisciplinary team teaching, flexible scheduling, and advisory programs have been suggested as ways to address adolescents' distinctive needs.

However, the effectiveness of these interventions—and all others—depends on whether they fit with a school's culture and leadership and how well they are implemented. In spite of their good intentions, few middle schools have implemented flexible scheduling. There is evidence that advisory programs and interdisciplinary team teaching are frequently enacted at only superficial levels, often because they require fundamental shifts in the beliefs and operating modes of schools and teachers. Thus, these strategies seem promising, but they are not easy to implement within current structures.

Academic Achievement

Detractors of middle schools point to the relatively poor standing of middle school students on international mathematics and science tests, to lagging test scores on state assessments, and to low performance on national tests as evidence that middle school education needs to be more challenging. In reality, the overall picture of middle school achievement is mixed.

International comparison studies show that the relative performance of U.S. students in mathematics and science declines from elementary school to middle school. National tests of achievement demonstrate that the majority of 8th graders fail to reach proficiency in mathematics, reading, and science. This is particularly true for African-Americans and Latinos, who continue to lag behind their white peers even when their parents have attained similar levels of education.

However, there has been overall improvement in standardized test scores in mathematics, science, and reading since the 1970s, and some score gaps between whites and other groups have narrowed. These results suggest that the efforts made thus far to improve achievement and to reduce performance gaps among different groups of students are at least somewhat successful.

Conditions That Affect Learning

Conditions for learning refers to the factors that can enhance or diminish a student's ability to learn. Particularly relevant for young teens are motivational and social-emotional indicators of well-being that are related to academic performance. Disengagement and social alienation are not only related to low achievement but also predict dropping out, whereas concerns about safety predict emotional distress that can compromise academic performance. Such findings underscore the need to examine a variety of student outcomes, in addition to academic indicators, for middle school students.

In our own analyses of international comparisons, based on the World Health Organization's (WHO's) Health Behavior of School Age Children (HBSC) survey, we compared different social-motivational indicators for U.S. middle school students to their same-age peers in 11 other countries. The comparisons show that U.S. students have negative perceptions of their learning conditions. These students rank the highest in terms of reported levels of emotional and physical problems and view the climate of their schools and the peer culture more negatively than do students in other countries.

Principals

Principals have potentially a great deal of influence on teachers' working conditions and on school climate and therefore also on the conditions that affect student learning. With data from the U.S. Department of Education Schools and Staffing Survey (SASS) of principals (SASS, 2001), we examined whether principals are spending time on the issues and activities deemed in the literature to be components of "good leadership."

While the literature identifies instructional leadership (that is, efforts to improve teaching) as being key, principals spend time on necessary administrative tasks, such as maintaining the physical security of their school, and on managing facilities, resources, and procedures. There is a disconnect between the more lofty goals articulated in the literature and the realities of the everyday tasks required of an effective operations manager.[1] This disconnect is especially problematic in light of the findings that suggest that the principal's support of reform designs (and presumably the time the principal is able to devote to providing support) is an important factor in whether school reforms are implemented.

Promoting Teacher Competence

Many middle school advocates believe that improving the education of middle school students hinges on improving the training of teachers. Much of the current policy debate related to middle schools concerns the lack of subject-matter expertise among teachers and a perceived need to have a separate middle school certification.

Only about one-quarter of middle school teachers are certified to teach at the middle grades; the majority of the rest are certified to teach at the elementary level. This means that teachers are likely to lack both subject-matter expertise and formal training on the development of young adolescents. Although improvements in professional development can potentially compensate for some of the inadequacies of preservice training, research suggests that professional development is often fragmented and unsystematic—that it is brief and lacks focus and alignment with standards.

---

[1] This finding could in part be due to the survey not asking about the specific kinds of issues identified in the literature.

Parental Involvement

Parental involvement takes many forms. Although it might be particularly effective for parents to be involved in the education of their young teens when they transition to middle school, parents tend to become less involved as children get older. Middle schools contribute to the decline in parental involvement by offering fewer activities and providing less support to parents than elementary schools do.

Whole-School Reforms

Most whole-school reforms targeted at the middle school level aim to improve student achievement through a variety of means, most commonly by increasing the competencies of teachers through professional development, by changing curriculum and instruction, and by enhancing classroom or school climate. As part of the federal government's Comprehensive School Reform effort, the reform models we discuss in this monograph show promise. Further research is needed not only to show whether these models fit all schools but also to show whether these reforms and their positive effects can be sustained over time.

Recommendations

We offer several recommendations to help meet the challenges identified above:

- Consider alternatives to the classic 6–8 grade middle school configuration that would reduce multiple transitions for students and allow schools to better align their goals across grades K–12.
- Offer interventions for the lowest-performing students, possibly including summer programs, before the 6th grade and additional reading and math courses, and tutorials after 6th grade to lessen the achievement gaps between certain demographic groups.
- Adopt comprehensive disciplinary models that focus on preventing disciplinary problems and changing the social norms or a peer culture that fosters antisocial behavior, and provide principals with technical assistance to support the cultural changes such models require.
- Make use of proven professional development models, to compensate for the lack of preservice training in subject-matter expertise and classroom management.
- Offer parents information about the academic and instructional goals and methods used in middle grades and suggest activities to facilitate learning at home.

- Establish a research program to learn how other countries successfully promote student well-being and foster positive school climates in a manner that supports academic achievement in schools that serve young teens.

In this monograph, we have attempted to integrate data and research on various aspects of middle schools to paint a comprehensive picture of teaching and learning in these schools. We have found that existing research is limited and that considerable information gaps exist. As we indicate throughout this monograph, additional studies in several areas could help answer many important questions and provide additional guidance to policymakers and practitioners.

Acknowledgements

We wish to thank the many individuals whose assistance was instrumental in conducting the reviews and analyses and in producing this monograph.

We are grateful to middle school researchers and advocates who shared their ideas and their work with us. Steven Mertens, in particular, provided feedback on an earlier draft of the monograph, and his thoughtful comments helped shape the final product.

At RAND, Sue Bodilly and Sheila Kirby have provided ongoing support since the earliest drafts. Laura Hamilton's careful and critical review improved the final version substantially. Shelley Wiseman worked closely with the authors, and her hard work pulling all the chapters together was substantial. We are grateful for the administrative help we received and want to thank the staff of RAND's Publications Department.

At UCLA, several students helped with various aspects of the research and the review process. We thank Christina Schofield, Melissa Witkow, Linda Issac, Nicole Nigosian, Kristen Seward, and Emily Vandever. Most importantly, thank you to Bernard Weiner for his thorough reviews and detailed feedback.

We appreciate the support that Mary Overpeck, Peter Scheidt, and Oddrun Samdal provided us in obtaining the World Health Organization data on Health Behavior of School Age Children for our analysis.

Finally, we recognize the energy and commitment of the teachers, principals, parents, and others who work with America's middle school students and help them have successful lives and fulfilling careers.

Abbreviations

AED	Academy for Education Development
AIM	AIM at Middle Grades Results
ATLAS	Authentic Teaching, Learning, and Assessment for All Students
CCD	Common Core of Data (U.S. Department of Education)
CMSA	Central Metropolitan Statistical Area
CSR	Comprehensive School Reform Program
DWOK	Different Ways of Knowing
GEAR UP	Gaining Early Awareness and Readiness for Undergraduate Programs
HBSC	Health Behavior of School Age Children
HS&B	High School and Beyond (a NELS study)
MMGW	Making Middle Grades Work
MSA	Metropolitan Statistical Area
NAEP	National Assessment of Educational Progress
NCES	National Center for Education Statistics (U.S. Department of Education)
NCLB	No Child Left Behind Act of 2001
NCREL	North Central Regional Educational Laboratory
NEA	National Education Association
NELS	National Education Longitudinal Study
NELS:88	National Education Longitudinal Study of 1988
NHES	National Household Education Survey
NLSAH	National Longitudinal Study of Adolescent Health
NMSA	National Middle School Association
OECD	Organization for Economic Cooperation and Development
OMB	Office of Management and Budget

PD	professional development
PISA	Programme International of Student Achievement
SASS	Schools and Staffing Survey
SES	socioeconomic status
SREB	Southern Regional Education Board
STEP	School Transitional Environment Project
TDMS	Talent Development Middle School Model
TIMSS	Third International Math and Science Study
TIMSS-R	TIMSS Repeat
TIPS	Teachers Involve Parents in Schoolwork
TPTMSM	Turning Points Transforming Middle Schools Model
UNICEF	United Nations Children's Fund
WHO	World Health Organization

CHAPTER ONE

Goals, Terms, Methods, and Organization

The Wonder Years, the sitcom that appeared on American television from 1988 to 1993, describes the problems and dreams of a suburban boy coming of age in the late 1960s and early 1970s. The boy's middle school years, as the show portrayed them, were believably complicated but "wonderful" nonetheless. Would a show about the experiences of young teens today paint the same picture? Can we rest easy knowing that the American middle school serves this population of students well?

The reputation of the American middle school today challenges any notion of "wonder years." Even the mildest public criticism acknowledges that "there is no denying that the 6th, 7th, and 8th graders present a unique set of challenges to students and teachers, from emerging hormones to widespread aggressiveness and regressing academic performances" ("Joel Klein's First Day of School," 2002). Critics have also described middle schools as the "Bermuda triangle of public education" ("Joel Klein's First Day of School," 2002) and middle school math and science as "an intellectual wasteland" (Schmidt, 2000). Middle schools are often blamed for the increase in behavioral problems among young teens and cited as the cause of teens' alienation, disengagement from school, and low achievement.

Purpose

A team of researchers from RAND Education set out to examine whether middle schools deserve their negative reputation. We collected and synthesized literature describing pertinent research conducted during the past 20 years. We identified not only critical issues indicated by the literature review but also issues that remain controversial and those that have not received much attention. We supplemented this review with our own analyses of the most recent and comprehensive national and international data. In describing our findings, this monograph

- identifies the major challenges U.S. middle schools face today
- describes current efforts to improve middle schools and evaluates the effectiveness of those efforts in light of existing research

- highlights the many areas lacking rigorous research focused specifically on middle schools
- suggests new ways of thinking about middle schools, middle school students, and middle school reform in light of history, research evidence, and current policy debates
- clarifies the priorities for those who must address the challenges U.S. middle schools face and, when possible, makes recommendations for next steps.

This book should be of interest to education policymakers and administrators at the national, state, district, and local levels; private advocacy and philanthropic organizations; teachers; parents; reformers and researchers.

Defining Our Terms

Today, over 15,000 of the more than 85,000 public schools in the United States serve nearly 9 million middle school age students. "Middle schools" most commonly begin with the 6th grade and end with the 8th grade, but some students in the "middle grades" are served in schools configured in other ways; for example, in schools serving grades 5 through 7 or in junior high schools with grades 7 and 8.

Education researchers and reformers often use the term *middle grades* to mean any range of grades from 5 to 8. In this report, we use the term *middle school* inclusively to refer to the intermediary phase of schooling that is separated administratively from elementary school and high school. Our analyses focus on *public* middle schools, although some studies and data sets (especially those that include nationally representative samples) also include private schools.

Figure 1.1 shows the four most prevalent grade configurations serving students in the middle grades in proportion to all schools (light bars) and to all students (dark bars), by locale. As shown in the figure, the 6-through-8 grade configuration is indeed the most common type of middle school across urban, suburban, and rural areas. (Appendix A provides more-detailed descriptions of school configurations, student-teacher ratios, and demographics.)

Methodology

The RAND team used a two-pronged methodology for the research and assessment that includes a comprehensive review of literature and analyses of nationally representative data.

Figure 1.1
Comparison of Different Middle School Grade Configurations Across Locales

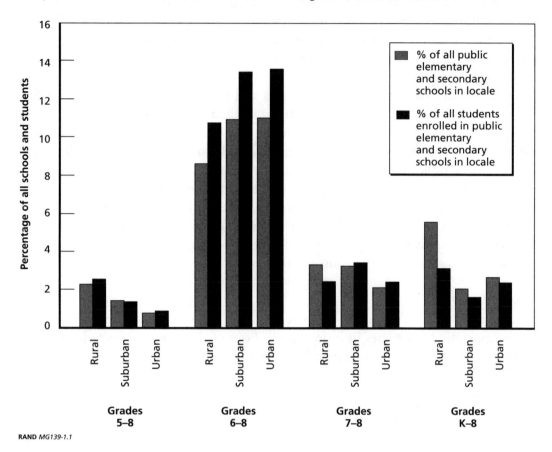

RAND *MG139-1.1*

The Literature Review

We began by reviewing a variety of standard databases, bibliographies, and similar sources to collect references on pertinent peer-reviewed articles, reports, monographs, and books, emphasizing research on middle schools from the past 20 years. Although our goal in the initial phase of this project was to be as inclusive as possible, we excluded work that was not broadly applicable.[1] The documents that were *not* selected (1) focused on narrow and/or tangential topics (for example, how best to design an athletic program), (2) were based on very small sample sizes (for example, case studies and samples with only a few students or just one classroom), or (3) were conducted abroad on topics not central to our work.

---

[1]Recent analyses by Hough (2003) show that the majority of research on middle schools has been published in the form of dissertations. He also shows that much of the empirical research is qualitative rather than quantitative and that much of the middle school literature can be classified as "scholarly writing," not empirical research.

After gathering, scanning, and organizing some 750 publications by topic, we winnowed the list of topics down to those we considered to be the most relevant. The team then asked experts both inside and outside RAND for feedback on which topics were critical to the debate and most relevant for our review. Further discussions with colleagues also helped us discover relevant unpublished studies to add to our literature review.

After we had narrowed down our topics and started reviewing relevant studies, we discovered that many of these investigations had been published in specialized journals geared for middle school practitioners. As a result, the majority of these studies did not provide the methodological details most research journals would include. For example, many investigations only summarized results. Few studies used methods that would account for differences in school or student characteristics. In some instances, studies lacked control groups, baseline data, and/or statistical controls. With these caveats in mind, we have relied on the best evidence available but recognize the tentativeness of the conclusions that we can draw, and we point to the limitations of the studies in the course of the text.

The Data Analyses

The data analyzed in this report are based on (but are not limited to) six data sets (which Appendix B describes in more detail). Four of these were collected under the auspices of the U.S. Department of Education and its National Center for Education Statistics (NCES):

- The Common Core of Data (CCD) is a nationally representative database of U.S. public elementary and secondary schools (Young, 2002). We used CCD data for 2000–2001 to compare schools with different grade configurations (5–8, 6–8, and 7–8) (see Appendix A).
- The National Assessment of Educational Progress (NAEP) provides continuing assessments of student knowledge and skills in a variety of subject areas. We used these data to describe historical trends in the achievement of U.S. 13-year-old students in science, mathematics, and reading and to compare the percentages of 8th-grade students reaching proficient levels of academic performance across different demographic groups (see Chapter Four).
- The National Education Longitudinal Study of 1988 (NELS:88) data (Carroll, 2000) collected a wide variety of data on a nationally representative sample of students in 1988, with later follow-ups with the respondents. We used these data to compare achievement gaps between white and African-American and white and Latino 8th-grade students in science, mathematics, and reading (see Chapter Four). We also refer to studies based on NELS:88 data in discussions

of other topics, such as middle school transition effects (Chapter Two) and parental involvement (Chapter Eight).[2]

- The Schools and Staffing Survey (SASS, 2001) focuses on teachers and administrators, gathering information on such things as staffing levels, hiring, and compensation; perceptions of school climate and problems; and school programs and student characteristics. We used these data to compare middle school teachers and principals with their elementary and high school colleagues. We also examined whether teacher and principal responses on the surveys varied across different types of middle schools (according to locale, ethnic composition, etc.). These findings are reported mainly in chapters Six and Seven, which focus on principals and teachers, respectively.

The other two data sets are international:

- The Third International Math and Science Study (TIMSS)[3] and its follow-up, TIMSS-Repeat (TIMSS-R), are intended to compare the abilities of U.S. and foreign students in these subjects (NCES, 2003). We used these data to describe the science achievement of U.S. 4th and 8th graders relative to their international peers from 37 nations (see Chapter Four).
- The World Health Organization's (WHO's) student survey of the Health Behavior of School Age Children (HBSC) has collected data on the physical, social, and emotional well-being of children since 1983–1984 (starting with 5 countries and growing to some 36 in 2001–2002 (WHO, 2002). We analyzed data from this resource for 12 countries that also have TIMSS-R data, which allowed us to compare U.S. middle school students with their peers in 11 Western nations (see Chapter Five).

We not only used these data to review findings from studies that have analyzed these data, we also conducted our own analyses using four of the data sets (HBSC; CCD; SASS; and, to a lesser degree, NELS:88).

Because we made a conscious decision to examine the big picture of U.S. middle schools and to elaborate on the challenges they face, our analyses rely on national and international data and do not include state-based achievement data. Although state-based data are valuable for some analyses, the differences across states and the idiosyncratic findings between state and national comparisons (for example, regard-

---

[2]NELS is an NCES program that was established to study the educational, vocational, and personal development of young people, beginning with their elementary or high school years and following them over time as they begin to take on adult roles and responsibilities. Thus far, the NELS program has consisted of three major studies: the National Longitudinal Study of the High School Class of 1972 (NLS-72), High School and Beyond (HS&B), and the National Education Longitudinal Study of 1988 (NELS:88).

[3]While this monograph was in preparation, the definition of TIMSS changed to Trends in International Mathematics and Science Study. We have, however retained the former meaning throughout.

ing the proportions of students deemed "proficient") complicate general conclusions. Such comparisons would not further the goals of our review.

Scope

As we were defining the scope of this monograph, it became apparent that we could not address all the issues that might be of interest to our audiences or that might merit further study. We had to make some difficult choices about how to limit the scope of our reviews.

We chose to devote a large part of the book to the key players—students, teachers, principals, and parents—who bear the brunt of the challenges that today's middle schools face and who are in a position to meet these challenges. Given that schools are evaluated according to student outcomes—academic achievement in particular—our primary emphasis is on students. However, student outcomes in part reflect teacher and principal effectiveness and parental support, as well as the teachers' instructional methods and the school's organizational features. We based our decisions about the inclusion of specific issues pertaining to principals, teachers, and parents partly on the current political debate (for example, whether teachers need to have separate middle school credentials) and partly on the amount and quality of the literature and data.

The challenges related to specific subject-matter content are beyond the scope of this book; indeed, each discipline deserves a book of its own. Similarly, the issues related to students with special needs (for example, students with limited English proficiency or with disabilities) are too complex and diverse to be included in this general overview. Also, we do not include analyses of financial constraints, although middle schools rely on many different sources of economic support, and funding issues are at the core of many of the challenges they face. This exclusion of topics does not imply that we do not regard them as important. These and other significant topics remain for subsequent work.

Organization

Chapter Two outlines a brief history of the American middle school and provides some perspective on the current criticisms and context for the issues that we tackle in the rest of the book. We describe the evolution of ideas and practices that define the current "middle school concept" in light of research findings conducted since the late 1970s. Chapter Three provides a more detailed description and assessment of the effectiveness of some of the core strategies of the middle school concept: interdisciplinary team teaching, advisory programs, and flexible block scheduling.

The next two chapters focus on students. Chapter Four examines middle school students' academic achievement in the nation as a whole, for subgroups of students, and for U.S. students compared with their peers internationally. Chapter Five reviews various "conditions for learning": factors that can enhance or diminish a student's ability to learn. Some of these conditions describe student characteristics, such as their psychosocial adjustment and physical health; others depict student perceptions of their school environment (for example, safety, social climate, and teacher support).

The next three chapters turn to the key players who are in a position to support young teens and shape their educational experience: principals, teachers, and parents. Chapter Six examines the challenges middle school principals face. Because previous research specifically on middle school principals has been limited, this chapter focuses primarily on the findings of our own analyses of the 2001 SASS data, the most recent available at the time. Chapter Seven reviews current policy debates about teacher qualifications and focuses on teacher training and professional development. Chapter Eight examines the role of parents in their children's schooling. Drawing on prior studies, we discuss the decline in parental involvement across grades and review what schools are doing—or not doing—to encourage parents to stay engaged in their children's education.

Chapter Nine describes six current, whole-school reform models.[4] We also review what is known about the effectiveness of these models. Chapter Ten highlights some of the current challenges U.S. middle schools face and makes recommendations for next steps.

We conclude with four appendixes. Appendix A describes the U.S. public school system. Appendix B describes the data sets we used here. Appendix C describes the factor analysis results for the HBSC data, and Appendix D offers recommendations for further research.

A Final Note

Each of the chapters in this monograph reviews the findings from our literature review in terms of their implications for U.S. middle schools. Each chapter has a conclusion that summarizes the major challenges and makes recommendations that follow from the research. We also explore some additional ideas and suggest alternative strategies that could help middle schools meet the challenges they face. We offer these ideas and strategies as examples to stimulate thinking but do not suggest that any of them is the only way to address the challenges facing middle schools.

---

[4] In this context, *whole-school* means engaging an entire school in a comprehensive reform.

To generate these exploratory ideas, we drew on the broad field of educational research, beyond that focused on middle schools. After all, many of the challenges middle schools face are not unique to grades 6 through 8. Many of the issues we raise can be addressed at different levels and by a variety of parties, including local associations, national organizations, private foundations, and federal and state governments. However, because many of the strategies we discuss have not yet been proven to be effective, we strongly recommend further testing and make specific suggestions for future research and evaluation.

CHAPTER TWO

A Brief History of the U.S. Middle School

To understand the challenges in today's middle schools, it is helpful to have some understanding of their history. This chapter provides a short description of the emergence of middle-grade education in the United States and shows how it has changed. We tell the story chronologically and, at the end of the chapter, summarize some common themes and suggest ways to apply the insights history provides to meeting today's challenges. Among the questions this chapter addresses are the following:

- What was the rationale for creating a separate level of schooling for young teens?
- How have middle school goals and educational practices evolved over time?
- What are the goals of the middle school concept that has emerged in over the past two decades?

From an "Eight-Four" to a "Six-Six" Grade Configuration

By 1900, the predominant school configuration in the United States consisted of eight years of primary school and four years of secondary school. However, according to educational historians (Beane, 2001; Brough, 1995; Cuban, 1992; Spring, 1986; Van Til, Vars, and Lounsbury, 1961), there were multiple societal pressures to reorganize this model at the turn of the century, including

- increased immigration, which burdened primary school enrollment in cities
- rapidly increasing industrialization and the need to prepare a better-educated workforce for the factories
- the demand from college presidents that college preparatory courses must start before the 9th grade (Eliot, 1898, cited in Brough, 1995).

These pressures created multiple and at times conflicting needs: accommodating large numbers of immigrant youth in urban schools, keeping students from dropping out, and preparing youth for the academic challenges of the high school and college curriculum.

In 1899, the National Education Association (NEA) published a report that argued for starting secondary education at the 7th rather than the 9th grade.

According to the report, "the seventh grade, rather than ninth, is the natural turning point in the pupil's life, as the age of adolescence demands new methods and wiser direction." The NEA's argument continued (NEA, 1899, p. 10):

> [T]he transition from elementary to the secondary period may be made natural and easy by changing gradually from the one-teacher regimen to the system of special teachers, thus avoiding the violent shock now commonly felt on entering the high school.

The NEA report was consistent with the work of an influential psychologist, Stanley Hall, who argued that unique developmental needs emerge during the time when youths reach puberty. In his classic book *Adolescence* (1905, p. 71), Hall describes a young teen:

> At dawning adolescence . . . this child is driven from his paradise and must enter upon a long viaticum of ascent, must conquer a higher kingdom of man for himself, break out a new sphere, and evolve a more modern story to his psychophysical nature.

He further provided a rationale for the specific educational needs of the age group (1905, p. 509):

> The pupil in the age of spontaneous variation which at no period of life is so great . . . suffers from mental ennui and dyspepsia, and this is why so many and an increasing number refuse some of the best prepared courses.

Although the 1899 NEA report provided a developmental rationale for the need to separate junior and senior levels of secondary schooling, it was not until later that the report was translated into concrete recommendations. The Committee on the Economy of Time and the Commission on the Reorganization of Secondary Education recommended in 1913 and in 1918, respectively, that secondary schools be divided into junior and senior levels. Yet, the first junior high schools (grades 7 and 8) had actually appeared by 1910 (Brough, 1995). Although the NEA recommendations played a part in this development, such historians as Beane (2001) and Cuban (1992) contend that societal and political pressures had the greatest influence on the creation of the junior high school.

The First Junior High Schools

Of all the societal changes, increased urbanization and immigration placed the most urgent demands on school systems, particularly on the new junior high schools (Van Til, Vars, and Lounsbury, 1961). Some of the specific concerns pertained to unsanitary living conditions in crowded urban ghettos and fear that immigrants were destroying traditional American values. Urban junior high schools provided health care facilities and education (Spring, 1986), as well as facilities (such as showers) and education to improve sanitary conditions. They created "Americanization programs" to help children assimilate culturally (Spring, 1986). The schools became critical community centers and social agencies serving not only the young but also their families.

In spite of the efforts of junior high schools to serve the needs of the rapidly changing society, only about one-third of students in public schools made it to 9th grade between 1907 and 1911 (Van Til, Vars, and Lounsbury, 1961). According to Brough (1995), several factors were blamed for the failure of students to progress to higher grades:

- abrupt transition
- irrelevance of the curriculum to the everyday lives of youths
- strict instruction
- the practice of retaining students when they did not meet the rigid requirements.

The Junior High Becomes the Middle School

In spite of the apparent failure of the new junior high schools, there was a sixfold increase in their number between 1922 and 1938 (Bossing and Cramer, 1965). Alexander and George (1981) attribute this rise partly to generally increasing enrollments following World War I. While the prevalence of junior high schools increased, there was also more discussion about the needs of the age group that these schools served. According to Brough (1995, p. 36), the "recognition of the uniqueness of the students provoked thought about uniqueness of the school program." Over time, the focus on the grade configuration was replaced in part by considerations about the educational functions of the junior high school. In the mid-1950s, Gruhn and Douglass (1956, p. 12) synthesized the "best thinking of the time" by emphasizing the following goals for the junior high school:

- *integration* of skills, interests, and attitudes that result in "wholesome pupil behavior"
- *exploration* of interests and abilities
- *differentiation* of educational opportunities based on student background, interests, and aptitudes
- *socialization* experiences that promote adjustment, guidance in decisionmaking
- *articulation* that assists youths in making the transition from an educational program designed for preadolescents to a program designed for adolescents.

In spite of the increased theoretical discussion about the educational goals and functions of the junior high schools, the schools themselves remained about the same. Dissatisfaction mounted in the 1960s as it became clear that the junior high continued to resemble the senior high school "with its emphasis on content rather than exploration, departmentalization rather than integration, and an adherence to rigid schedule" (Brough, 1995, p. 38). At the same time, secondary school enrollments were declining, and elementary school enrollments, in contrast, were expanding both because of larger birth cohorts and the increasing popularity of early childhood education and kindergartens. According to Alexander (1984), the resulting shortage of space at the elementary level caused the 6th grade to be pushed out into the junior high level.

Several societal changes, including the civil rights movement, also affected the speed of school reorganization efforts. By 1971, many school desegregation plans involved reorganization of the middle grades (Brough, 1995). According to Alexander and McEwin (1989), the number of U.S. 7–8 grade junior high schools decreased from 4,711 to 2,191 between 1970 and 1986, while the number of 6–8 grade middle schools increased from 1,662 to 4,329.

Although space considerations and other logistics were influencing the configuration of the schools, new research was showing that young teens of the 1960s were reaching puberty earlier than their peers had in the early 1900s (Tanner, 1962). Not unlike the work of Hall (1905), these findings about young teens' biological maturity seemed to support earlier transfer from elementary schools. However, a 1967 survey of middle school principals reported that the most frequent reason for establishing middle schools had to do with relieving crowded conditions in other schools (Alexander and George, 1981). Thus, enrollment pressures and larger societal issues were important in shaping the formation of middle schools for grades 6–8 from the beginning of the 1900s through the 1960s.

A Middle School Concept Emerges in the 1980s

The discussion of and scholarly writing about the needs of young adolescents that began in the late 1970s heightened during the 1980s (Dickinson, 2001). In their landmark book, *The Exemplary Middle School*, Alexander and George (1981, p. 2) wrote about a new philosophy of how middle schools should work, presenting a new middle school concept.

> The concept of a bridging school is not enough, however, because children of middle school age have their unique characteristics and needs which cannot be subordinated to the impact of the elementary school nor to the demands of the high school. An effective middle school must not only build upon the program on earlier childhood and anticipate the program of secondary education to follow, but it must be directly concerned with the here-and-now problems and interests of its students. Furthermore, the middle school should not be envisioned

as a passive link in the chain of education below the college and university, but rather as a dynamic force in improving education.

As new paradigms for reforming middle-grade education were brewing in the early 1980s, middle school researchers, educators, and advocates voiced concerns about society's lack of attention to young teens. For example, in her book called *Growing Up Forgotten*, Lipsitz (1980) noted that this age group was underserved. In the 1980s, the vulnerability of young adolescents and the disturbing statistics on their drug use and precarious sexual behavior caught the attention of policymakers, as well the public at large. Critics challenged middle schools to care about the "whole child." Not surprisingly, there were efforts to make schools—especially those that served "at-risk" youth—into full-service community centers that could facilitate the development of young teens (for example, Dryfoos, 1995; McMahon et al., 2000). This idea was not unlike the one that had shaped the urban junior high schools that immigrant youth attended in the early 1900s. Such recycling of priorities is not uncommon for educational reform (Tyack and Cuban, 1995).

The Transition as Culprit

Research during the 1980s suggested that the *timing* of the transition to junior high school, during the onset of puberty, was particularly disruptive for youth. Simmons and Blyth (1987) compared students across two different school configurations: 7th graders who made the transition to junior high school in the beginning of 7th grade and 7th graders who remained in a K–8 school. The findings of the study showed that 7th graders in the new school environment were worse off than the same-age peers who remained in the K–8 school. The 7th graders who transitioned to a new school had lower self-esteem, had more negative attitudes about school, and received lower grades. Eccles, Lord, and Midgley (1991) subsequently replicated these findings by using NELS data to compare 8th grade students who attended K–8 schools with those who attended schools having other configurations.[1] In addition to temporary transition effects, Simmons and Blyth (1987) showed that students' problems during the transition to junior high school predicted other problems during high school.

Reviewing the research of the 1970s and 1980s, Eccles and Midgley (1989) documented that the transition to junior high or middle school was marked by general declines in student motivation, attitude about school, perception of ability, and academic achievement. The researchers proposed that these findings supported the idea that it was the *nature* of the transition that caused problems. Specifically, they contended that there was a poor fit between the developmental needs of young teens

---

[1]Other, more general evidence also suggests that transitions are marked by achievement losses (Alspaugh, 1998), especially when they include a change from self-contained to departmentalized classrooms (Alspaugh and Harting, 1995).

(for example, the need to have stable and close relationships) and the environmental changes related to the transition from elementary schools to junior high or middle school (new teachers and less-personal relationships with them). Table 2.1 summarizes some of the school-related changes Eccles and colleagues identified.

According to Eccles and her colleagues, young teens undergo these changes in the school environment just as they are going through major social, psychological, physical and cognitive changes. The researchers argued that these changes decreased the fit between the student and the school environment. For example, young teens want to become more autonomous, but their teachers become more rather than less controlling. Also, the grading practices were shown to become stricter and more competitive as young teens are becoming increasingly self-conscious. Eccles and her colleagues proposed that the poor match between developmental needs and the changes in the school environment decreased motivation, self-esteem, and academic performance.

Carnegie Report Elaborates on Mismatch Concept

Guided by the findings of research in the 1980s, the Carnegie Council on Adolescent Development presented a powerful vision for middle schools with its 1989 report, *Turning Points: Preparing American Youth for the 21st Century*. This report emphasized both the perils young teens face and the potential they could reach. The council concluded with the following (Carnegie, 1989, p. 32):

> Middle grade schools—junior high, intermediate, or middle schools—are potentially society's most powerful force to recapture millions of youth adrift. Yet too often they exacerbate the problems the youth face. A volatile mismatch exists between the organization and curriculum of middle grades schools, and the intellectual, emotional, and interpersonal needs of young adolescents.

Using the conceptual model of a mismatch between developmental stage and environment, the council presented ways to bridge the gap or to facilitate matching young adolescents' needs, capabilities, and learning environments. The Carnegie report identified five broad goals for the education of young teens. These goals reflected some of the same notions of "wholesome pupil behavior" that Gruhn and Douglass (1956) had put forth 40 years before. Specifically, the report proposed that a 15-year-old student graduating from middle school ought to be (1) an intellectually reflective person, (2) a person en route to a lifetime of meaningful work, (3) a good citizen, (4) a caring and ethical individual, and (5) a healthy person. To accomplish these goals, the council made eight recommendations for improving education during the middle grades:

- dividing large middle schools into smaller communities of learning
- teaching all students a core of common knowledge
- ensuring success for all students

- empowering teachers and administrators
- preparing teachers for the middle grades
- improving academic performance through better health and fitness
- reengaging families in the education of young adolescents
- connecting schools with communities.

Although many of these recommendations were consistent with the reform efforts of the 1950s, there was one exception: Gruhn and Douglass (1956) had proposed that educational opportunities differ according to the student's background, interests, and aptitudes (Brough, 1995), but the Carnegie council endorsed a core of common knowledge for all.[2]

The council identified specific strategies for achieving these goals (Chapter Three provides a more-detailed discussion). For example, the Carnegie council proposed teaming teachers and students to facilitate closer teacher-student relationships. Similarly, it proposed that classroom advisory programs would allow teachers to provide much-needed guidance and support for developing young teens. It suggested that an interdisciplinary curriculum would facilitate critical thinking at the time when young teens are becoming better able to comprehend connections and the relationships between various topics and issues.

Table 2.1
The Transition from Elementary School to Middle School

	Elementary School	Junior High or Middle School
Environmental changes	Small schools Oldest in the school One or two teachers, close relationship Same classroom with same classmates	Large schools Youngest in the school Many teachers, distant relationships Changing classrooms from one period to another
Changes in teaching practices	Smaller classes with opportunities for decisionmaking Small group and individual instruction Mix of abilities in each class Learning opportunities that demand higher-order cognitive processes	Greater emphasis on teacher control and discipline; fewer decisionmaking opportunities for students Whole-class instruction Increased between-class ability grouping Less cognitively demanding tasks (for example, drill), yet stricter evaluation criteria

SOURCES: Eccles and Midgley (1989) and Eccles, Lord, and Midgley (1991).

---

[2]This change might in part reflect the more-recent emphasis on social equity that underlies the efforts to abolish academic tracking (for example, by the National Association for Accelerated Middle School Reform; see Chapter Nine).

Developmental Responsiveness in the 1990s

In the 1990s, *developmental responsiveness* frequently referred, in practice, to students' social-emotional needs, not to the need for more cognitively challenging tasks. There was substantial emphasis on how to facilitate closer teacher-student relationships and how to make middle schools feel more personal (Lipsitz, Jackson, and Austin, 1997). It is not clear whether there was greater emphasis on social-emotional needs than on cognitive needs or whether it was simply easier to improve the social climate and student-teacher relationships than to change instructional strategies. There is some evidence that fostering advisor-advisee programs, linking students with teacher mentors, and grouping students into smaller units (teams) have improved both students' perceptions of the support they obtain from teachers and their general feelings of connectedness (Felner, Jackson, et al., 1997). However, there has also been a growing consensus that, although these feelings are associated with higher academic performance among middle school students (Goodenow, 1993), changes in the social climate are not sufficient to improve achievement (Lipsitz, Mizell, et al., 1997; Williamson and Johnston, 1999).

The mismatch between increased *cognitive* capabilities (improved memory and reasoning abilities) and lower-level instructional strategies (for example, emphasizing rote learning) that such researchers as Eccles and Midgley (1989) pointed out did not receive widespread attention. Reviews of studies from the 1970s and 1980s suggested that, although students' cognitive capabilities improved during the middle grades in terms of their ability to think abstractly, consider different perspectives, and take multiple factors into account at once (Keating, 1990), the instructional strategies became less cognitively demanding. For example, Rounds and Osaki (1982) showed that the work required in the first year of middle school was less demanding than that of the last year of elementary school (see also Center for Research on Elementary and Middle Schools, 1990). Similarly, Schmidt and Valverde (1997) noted that many of the mathematics and science topics that are part of the core curricula during the elementary years are also covered in the middle grades, resulting in middle school curricula that are undemanding and repetitive. Thus, it is not surprising that transferring to middle school may undermine students' motivation and possibly also their academic performance.

Although the changes in the school environment are presumed to contribute to negative outcomes for adolescents, the causal relationship has not been tested explicitly. For example, in a longitudinal study, Midgley and Feldaufer (1987) demonstrated that the mismatch between adolescents' ability to make decisions and the decisionmaking opportunities afforded to them increased after their transition to middle school and presumed that this mismatch decreased students' motivation (see also Gentry, Gable, and Rizza, 2002). However, the link to loss of motivation has not been tested explicitly.

Role of Professional Organizations

Other potent forces besides conceptual models have also guided the middle school movement. George (1999) calls the middle school movement one of the strongest grass-roots reform movements in the United States. Indeed, since 1982, the National Middle School Association (NMSA) has published a series of position papers called "This We Believe." NMSA (1995, pp. 10–11) identified six prerequisites for developmentally responsive schools:

- educators committed to young adolescents
- a shared vision
- high expectations for all
- an adult advocate for every student
- family-community partnerships
- a positive school climate.

NMSA (1995, pp. 10–11) further identified six components that need to be implemented for schools to be developmentally responsive:

- curriculum that is challenging, integrative, and exploratory
- varied teaching and learning approaches
- assessment and evaluation that promote learning
- flexible organizational structures
- programs and policies that foster health, wellness, and safety
- comprehensive guidance and support services.

It is difficult to disagree with these recommendations. Yet it is not always clear *how* to reach the goals or how the specific goals and practices are linked.

Recent Debates and Research Findings

One of the presumed key functions of middle schools, bridging, requires aligning the transitions both *to* and *from* middle school with the goals of elementary and high schools, respectively. Making these alignments is challenging because the problems associated with the transition from elementary school are considered mainly social-emotional (for example, increasingly anonymous school environment, distant relationships with extrafamilial adults, and interruptions in peer networks), but the problems related with the transition to high school are considered academic. The academic problems associated with the transition to high school have received increased attention recently (for example, Bottoms, Cooney, and Carpenter, 2003).

In the policy debate, different goals or priorities for guiding middle school reform are often pitted against one another. Practitioners and researchers alike ask whether, in terms of achievement, developmentally sensitive practices that emphasize the social-emotional well-being of students matter more than those that emphasize academic rigor (for example, Phillips, 1997). Yet some of the latest research (Lee and Smith, 1999; Lee, Smith, et al., 1999) suggests that students do best in educational settings that provide social support *and* emphasize academic rigor.

Lee and Smith (1999) examined the effects on achievement of the support students receive from teachers, parents, peers, and neighborhoods (as reported by students). The researchers examined 6th through 8th graders in 304 Chicago K–8 public schools that varied in the degree to which the school mission focused on learning and the degree to which students reported that teachers challenged them to do well. The researchers found that students who felt supported and were in schools that emphasized academic rigor showed the largest gains in achievement in 6th and 8th grades.

A balance between support and academic rigor is indeed one of the goals of many of today's middle school reform efforts (see Chapter Nine). They aim to achieve this balance by applying the practices that help create smaller learning communities in which teachers know their students and in which students' academic progress can be carefully monitored.

Challenges, Recommendations, and Exploratory Ideas

Our historical review shows that many of today's concerns about young teens and the proper way to educate them are similar to the concerns that have been expressed for the past 100 years. These goals have included the need to (1) provide an education for all, (2) address young teens' developmental uniqueness, (3) serve the whole person (and even the whole family and community), and (4) impose high academic standards on students and prepare them for high school and college. However, the solutions that are endorsed at a given time often have more to do with problems related not to education but to a variety of societal and practical issues, such as overcrowding in school buildings. *Thus, throughout the history of the American middle school, the creation of separate schools for young adolescents has been guided primarily by pragmatic concerns.*

The only scientifically based argument for separating young teens from their younger peers relied on research on pubertal development. Early 20th-century research describing developing teens indicated that they would be best served in separate schools. Yet researchers in the late 1970s and early 1980s came to a different conclusion: Young teens suffered from the abruptness of the transition from elementary school. These studies also suggested that *the onset of puberty is an especially poor reason for beginning a new phase of schooling, inasmuch as multiple simultaneous changes (for example, the onset of puberty and school transfer) are stressful and sometimes have long-lasting negative effects.*

The few studies that compared schools with different grade configurations suggest that young teens do better in K–8 schools than in configurations that require a transition to a different school. *In light of this evidence and the historical reasons for the separation of the junior high school from the senior high school, we challenge the rationale of a separate middle school.*

Although the old K–8 configuration might serve students well, it is not necessarily the only option. The structure or configuration of the school that serves middle grades could remain flexible as long as the number of transitions is reduced and changes in the size and structure of schools, curriculum, and instruction are introduced gradually. For example, rather than going from self-contained classrooms to different teachers for all or most subjects at once, why not gradually introduce subject-matter specialists across grades 3–6?

Alternative models for middle grades education have been explored mostly in the context of traditional structures or configurations (see Chapter Nine). Yet, many promising organizational features and instructional practices might be easier to implement and sustain in some types of structure than in others. For example, Hough (1995) has argued that it may be easier to foster many of the trademark practices of middle schools within "elemiddle" schools, schools combining elementary and middle grades. *We strongly encourage evaluation of alternative models for middle grades—models that do not require multiple transitions, allow better coordination of goals across grades K–12, and can foster academic rigor as well as provide social support.*

CHAPTER THREE

Core Practices of the Middle School Concept

In our brief history of the U.S. middle school in Chapter Two, we described the emergence in the early 1980s of a new concept for middle schools. Part of this new concept was a recognition that the needs of young teens are different from those of elementary and high school students and that middle schools should be organized in such a way that the students' developmental needs are met. Today's concerns about students' academic achievement have led to increased scrutiny of middle schools and have fueled ongoing debates about the proper role, structure, and organization of middle schools.

Guided by the notion of a developmental mismatch between the needs of young teens and their middle school environments, some researchers have hypothesized that developmentally inappropriate practices underlie the declines in students' motivation and achievement (Anderman and Maehr, 1994; Eccles and Midgley, 1989; Wigfield, Eccles, and Pintrich, 1996). Middle school reformers and advocates have recommended a number of practices to ameliorate this mismatch.

This chapter describes practices designed to be responsive to the developmental needs of young teens that could be considered hallmarks of the middle school concept introduced in the 1980s (for example, Alexander and George, 1981). We mainly focus on three practices at the core of middle school ideology: (1) interdisciplinary team teaching, (2) flexible scheduling, and (3) advisory programs. Although other instructional and organizational practices have been designed to improve the development of teens in middle schools, we focus on these three because they are frequently mentioned in the literature and are promoted by leading middle school organizations, including the Carnegie Council on Adolescent Development, NMSA, and the National Forum to Accelerate Middle School Reform. We include a brief discussion of *looping*—the practice of keeping groups of students together for two or more years with the same teacher—as an example of more-recent efforts to be responsive to teens' developmental needs.

This chapter addresses the following questions, among others:

- What is the underlying rationale for each of the core practices?
- How extensively are they implemented in today's schools?

- What do we know about their effectiveness?

In assessing effectiveness in light of the available data, we focus mainly on student achievement. We also distinguish between "promising" and "proven" practices. *Promising* efforts are those for which the positive evidence is limited—in the sense that there are only a few studies on the topic and that they have limited generalizability across schools, districts, and states. We also consider instructional and organizational practices promising when positive effects are obtained by relying on research designs or methods that lack appropriate comparison groups or statistical controls (for example, prior levels of achievement when examining improvement in achievement). A *proven* practice, in contrast, is one that has been experimentally tested with representative samples and has been shown to be superior.

When evaluating the effectiveness of instructional and organizational strategies promoted for middle schools, it is important to recognize that some of these ideas, such as advisory programs, were proposed to facilitate closer relationships between teachers and students, not necessarily to improve achievement directly. With the current emphasis on accountability and achievement (especially as a result of the No Child Left Behind Act of 2001 [NCLB]), such middle school practices are receiving considerable scrutiny, and policymakers and practitioners are looking for evidence about their effectiveness in increasing achievement.

Interdisciplinary Team Teaching

George and Alexander (1993), p. 249, defined *interdisciplinary team teaching* as

> a way of organizing the faculty so that a group of teachers share: (1) the same group of students; (2) the responsibility for planning, teaching, and evaluating curriculum and instruction in more than one academic area; (3) the same schedule; and (4) the same area of the building.

A key component of interdisciplinary team teaching is *common planning time*; members of a teaching team have the same free period, in which they can plan, coordinate, and discuss curricular issues and students' needs together.

Muth and Alverman (1992) describe three advantages of interdisciplinary teaching for students. First, because teachers share the same groups of students, they can discuss the strengths and weaknesses of individual students, making it easier to meet their needs. Second, interdisciplinary teams of teachers can facilitate connections across different disciplines. Finally, there are more opportunities for positive peer and teacher-student relationships because teachers on the same team teach the same groups of students.[1]

---

[1] For a summary of the benefits of interdisciplinary teaming on teachers and student perceptions of belonging and engagement, see Arhar (1992, 1997).

Although interdisciplinary team teaching is not always implemented with common planning time, research has found that teams that do are more likely to engage in team activities than those that do not (Flowers, Mertens, and Mulhall, 2000; Warren and Muth, 1995). Whether or not common planning time is provided, interdisciplinary team teaching is practiced in some form or another in many middle schools today. According to a recent survey, 79 percent of responding middle school principals (only 6.5 percent of those surveyed responded) indicated that their schools had implemented interdisciplinary teams (Valentine, Clark, et al., 2002). We presume that this is an overestimate, not only because of the biased sample but also because the 79-percent estimate could also reflect occasional collaboration between two teachers (for example, coteaching one particular unit).

Empirical studies of the effects of interdisciplinary team teaching have reported positive achievement results for students. Russell (1997) found that interdisciplinary teaming (in conjunction with other middle school program concepts) was positively associated with gains on 8th-grade reading and mathematics scores. Using a subset of NELS:88 data, Lee and Smith (1993) found that students in middle schools that implemented programs consistent with the middle school concept, such as less departmentalization and more team teaching (which are good proxies for interdisciplinary team teaching), had higher academic achievement and engagement than students in more-traditional schools. Other studies have confirmed that outcomes depend on the level of implementation (Felner et al., 1997).

Mertens, Flowers, and Mulhall (1998) reported on a reform effort, the Middle Start Initiative, which aimed to increase the implementation of certain recommended middle school practices, including interdisciplinary team teaching. Mertens, Flowers, and Mulhall found that higher percentages of students in schools that had implemented interdisciplinary team teaching at a high level (that is, had common planning time) achieved a "satisfactory" performance level on the statewide achievement test than did those in schools with low levels or no implementation.[2]

For the most part, studies on interdisciplinary team teaching are difficult to interpret because this instructional approach is often implemented concurrently with other middle school practices, making it difficult to disentangle the separate effects of each practice (Van Zandt and Totten, 1995). Additionally, many of the studies examining the effects of interdisciplinary team teaching on students (for example, Lee and Smith, 1993) had data limitations, such as a lack of test scores prior to the 8th grade. Thus, the results might also reflect preexisting differences in student achievement. It is conceivable that schools with high-achieving students are more likely to use nontraditional instructional approaches.

Similarly, Mertens, Flowers, and Mulhall (1998) presented tabulations of achievement results by implementation level (grouping the schools according to how

---

[2] See also Felner et al. (1997) and Flowers, Mertens, and Mulhall (1999).

extensively interdisciplinary team teaching had been implemented), but implementation level was related to school demographics. Schools that had implemented interdisciplinary team teaching at a higher level also tended to serve fewer students eligible for free- or reduced-price lunches. Thus, it is unclear to what extent the association between interdisciplinary team teaching and higher student achievement was attributable to implementation level or to demographic differences. Although three high-poverty, high-implementing schools showed greater gains than did more affluent, lower-implementing schools, it is unclear how generalizable these findings are across schools that serve large numbers of poor students.

Additional research is needed to show whether most schools can implement interdisciplinary team teaching at a high-enough level to be effective, but the evidence thus far suggests that it is a *promising* practice for improving student achievement in middle grades. What we do not know is whether interdisciplinary team teaching is superior to other instructional innovations. We return to this question at the end of the chapter in discussing the challenges of getting teachers to work together across disciplines.

Flexible Scheduling

In an attempt to move away from a traditional structure in which the school day is organized around a discrete number of periods with fixed lengths, middle school advocates recommend flexible scheduling. Flexible scheduling entails alterations in "the school day schedule from several equally divided periods to a format that provides fewer, but longer flexible periods" (Brown, 2001, p. 129). Other alternative scheduling formats are intended to provide more flexibility than the traditional period-by-period schedule (Valentine and Whitaker, 1997). These include "alternating-day block schedules" (students attend four class periods for the entire school year, but each class meets every other day) or "4 x 4 plans" (students attend four class periods that meet every day for one semester, but begin four new class periods at the start of the next semester). Although these plans are more flexible than traditional scheduling, they still consist of periods of fixed length, usually 60 to 90 minutes, which cannot be adjusted even when learners or instructors need more time in a given situation (Brown, 2001, p. 130). True flexible scheduling can be distinguished from other alternative formats because it is not demarcated by periods of fixed length.

The primary rationale supporting the use of flexible scheduling relates to the quality of student learning. For example, Kauchak and Eggen (1998) contend that activities that emphasize problem-solving or critical thinking require more time, which a traditional period-by-period schedule does not accommodate. Extended learning periods also give students time to make connections across different disciplines (Beane, 1993; Perkins, 1992). Additionally, longer periods allow more opportunities for interaction among students and between teachers and students, which can improve interpersonal relationships (NMSA, 1995).

Rettig and Canady (2000) estimate that flexible scheduling may be the least implemented of the innovations commonly advocated for middle schools. Indeed, Valentine, Clark, et al. (2002) report that the traditional period-by-period format is the most common schedule. Hence, it is not surprising that we were unable to locate any empirical studies that have examined the effect of flexible scheduling on student performance.

Despite the lack of empirical studies on the effects of flexible scheduling on student outcomes, we may be able to gauge its possible effects indirectly by examining some of the empirical studies that have compared the achievement results of students in traditional scheduling formats with students in other alternative scheduling formats. The findings of these studies have been inconsistent, with some reporting higher gains for students in alternative schedules (Thayer and Shortt, 1999), others reporting no differences (Schroth and Dixon, 1996), and still others reporting losses compared with students in traditional schedules (Cobb, Abate, and Baker, 1999). Given that these studies examined various forms of alternative schedules and not flexible scheduling per se, it remains unclear what kinds of effects flexible scheduling can have on student motivation and learning.

Moreover, the low frequency of implementation and the lack of studies on this topic are also telling. Flexible scheduling might be particularly difficult to implement in large, crowded schools. Thus, this practice is unlikely to survive under the daily constraints of many middle schools.

Advisory Programs

In light of calls that "every student needs to have a relationship with at least one adult in the school which is characterized by warmth, concern, openness and understanding" (George and Alexander, 1993, p. 201), such prominent organizations as the National Association of Secondary School Principals and the Carnegie Council on Adolescent Development have endorsed advisory programs. Advisory programs are arrangements in which adults meet regularly with groups of students to mentor, guide, and provide support. Although different types of advisory programs have varying objectives, most aim to promote smaller communities of learners and provide individual attention to students (Anafra and Brown, 2001). A more positive psychosocial climate, in turn, can enhance student learning (Goh, 1995). Thus, advisory programs differ slightly from the other two practices discussed above because they are not intended to affect student achievement directly.

Although 57 percent of responding middle school principals indicated that their schools had regularly scheduled advisory programs (Valentine, Clark, et al., 2002), there is evidence that advisory programs and interdisciplinary team teaching are often enacted only superficially (MacIver and Epstein, 1991). Furthermore, little is known about the programs' effectiveness. Felner et al. (1993) studied advisory programs as part of the School Transitional Environment Project (STEP), an intervention that restructured schools to ease the transition as students moved into middle and high schools. After controlling for various student background characteristics, Felner et al. (1993) concluded that students in the STEP program were more likely to report positive perceptions of the school climate, including fewer negative student interactions and more teacher support, than did their peers in non-STEP schools.

Studying the effects of advisory programs in a middle school three years after the programs had been implemented, Ziegler and Mulhall (1994) reported that the majority of students felt that advisory groups strengthened the bond between teachers and students. Similarly, in a large-scale survey of approximately 3,400 7th graders, Putbrese (1989) found that students in advisory programs reported higher levels of satisfaction with student-teacher and peer relationships than did students not enrolled in advisory programs. Finally, after controlling for differences in grade configurations and in student, school, and regional characteristics, MacIver and Epstein (1991) reported that principals who had enacted advisory programs expected lower dropout rates than did those who did not have advisory programs in place.

As Galassi, Gulledge, and Cox (1997) point out in their comprehensive review of advisory programs, the studies on advisories had methodological limitations. Advisory programs, for example, were just one feature of the STEP intervention as described in Felner et al. (1993). Therefore, it is unclear to what extent the positive outcomes could be attributed specifically to the advisory component of the intervention as opposed to other features. Because the Ziegler and Mulhall (1994) study lacked baseline data, it is possible that positive relationships existed in the sample schools before the implementation of the advisory programs. In the Putbrese (1989) study, differences between schools with and without advisory programs might have reached statistical significance yet still have been very small, given the large sample size. Additionally, MacIver and Epstein (1991) does not make clear whether the dropout rates the principals had predicted corresponded with the eventual actual rates. Taken together, the findings suggest that advisory programs represent a promising but not proven practice to promote positive school climate.

A More Recent Practice: Looping

Among the other practices that advocates promote for supporting the broad goals of the middle school concept, looping is one of the more recent. The idea behind looping is that keeping groups of students together for two or more years with the same teacher will improve teacher-student relationships and the teachers' ability to recognize their students' academic strengths and weaknesses (Black, 2000). Despite the intuitive appeal of looping and its apparent potential for maintaining continuity of experience for young teens, only 17 percent of teachers in our SASS analyses indicated that their schools used this practice.[3]

A limited number of studies attest to the benefits. Comparing the social relations and academic achievement of middle school students in looped and nonlooped classes, Lincoln (1998) found that looped classes had advantages with respect to test scores, self-efficacy, and attitudes toward schools. Similarly, Grant (2000) reported on a Massachusetts district that used looping for students in 1st through 8th grades. Research over a seven-year period found that, after the implementation of looping, student attendance and retention rates increased, disciplinary actions and suspensions decreased, and staff attendance improved. Thus, based on a very limited research base, looping appears to be another promising practice. How well this practice would be implemented across many schools on a larger scale is not known.

Obstacles for Implementation

Interdisciplinary team teaching; flexible scheduling; advisory programs; and more recently, looping have been suggested as ways to address the developmental needs of young teens. These strategies have sound rationales, and research results thus far suggest that several of these practices hold some promise for improving student achievement or school climate. However, the effectiveness of these efforts—and all others—depends on how well they are implemented.

One of the biggest challenges in implementing educational reforms is altering the traditional ways teachers behave (Cuban, 1992). For example, to implement interdisciplinary team teaching, teachers from different disciplines must work closely together. Many teachers, however, prefer the conventional structure because departmental affiliation is important to their professional identity (Lee and Smith, 1993). Other teachers prize their individual classroom autonomy and view collaboration as an infringement on their independence (Brown, 2001). Teachers also resist change because they do not know how to collaborate with other teachers across different departments, and few in-service training programs focus on this aspect of pedagogy (Hutcheson and Moeller, 1995).

The success of the middle school concept depends not only on teachers but also on the school structure. For example, interdisciplinary team teaching requires schools to allow teachers time both for individual planning and to work together with teach-

---

[3] For more on our analyses of SASS, see p. 6 and Chapters Six and Seven of this volume.

ers from different departments to plan and discuss student and curriculum issues (Howe and Bell, 1998). Because most schools schedule only individual planning time (McEwin, Dickinson, and Swaim, 1996), the burden falls on teachers to find time to collaborate with one another. The traditional period-by-period school day structure decreases the chances that members of an interdisciplinary team will have the same preparation period. In Chapter Nine, we discuss ways to conduct the necessary comprehensive restructuring.

Although comprehensive reform models may provide more-ideal conditions for nontraditional instructional and organizational practices to work, changing a school's structure can also have some unintended consequences. For example, some evidence suggests that changes in the departmental structure of schools can decrease teachers' subject-matter expertise (McPartland, 1991), because teachers in the same discipline have fewer opportunities to share ideas about their field. Given that studies have found that students whose teachers had more subject-matter knowledge performed higher on standardized achievement tests than did those whose teachers had less (Darling-Hammond, 2000; Monk, 1994), it is important to understand whether eliminating "walls" between departments can have unintended negative consequences.

Challenges, Recommendations, and Exploratory Ideas

Because evidence about how the middle school concept operates at the school level is limited (Mitman, Lash, and Mergendeller, 1985), it is difficult to offer school professionals definitive answers about the effectiveness of the practices. We do not know, for example, how applicable different organizational and instructional practices are in all contexts, or whether all schools can successfully implement them without substantial resources over time. It may well be that many of the developmentally responsive practices are ideal but can be put into practice only under unique or specialized conditions (Cuban, 1992). *Full implementation of interdisciplinary team teaching and other features of the middle school concept may require comprehensively restructuring schools to support these practices.*

Although many factors, including structural features, can explain the reluctance of schools to adopt these practices or their tendency to adopt them only superficially, we presume that another important reason is that many of the proposed practices require schools and teachers to make fundamental shifts in their beliefs and operating modes. For example, teachers are not used to working together across disciplinary lines. Shifts in modes and models of behavior require opportunities to model, experiment, obtain feedback, and reflect. Thus, new practices are unlikely to flourish without teacher professional learning opportunities and without structural and resource support.

CHAPTER FOUR

Academic Achievement

As Chapter Two reviewed, middle schools have shifted focus several times between academic achievement and meeting the social, emotional, and psychological needs of early adolescents. In recent years, the pendulum has swung back toward achievement. This emphasis has been further reinforced by the standards and accountability movement and NCLB, the 2001 federal legislation that mandates testing of all students in the middle grades and imposes sanctions on schools designated as "low performing."

As before, today's focus on achievement stems in part from the belief that middle school students should begin to think about and prepare for college (Riley, 1997). Such programs as the federally funded Gaining Early Awareness and Readiness for Undergraduate Programs (GEAR UP) earmark funds and services for low-income middle schools in an effort to increase the number of students who are prepared to enter and succeed in postsecondary education. Increased attention on achievement also stems from mounting criticism levied at middle schools for being academically undemanding (Carnegie, 1989; Jackson and Davis, 2000; Schmidt, McKnight, et al., 1999; Cooney, 1998a). Detractors point to the relatively poor standing of middle school students on international mathematics and science tests, to lagging test scores on state assessments, and to low performance on national tests as evidence that middle school education needs to be more challenging.

The goal of this chapter is to assess the accuracy of the often-publicized accounts of unacceptably low achievement of middle school students. We review achievement data by relying on various comparisons across nations, over time, and among some key demographic groups. Among the questions we address are the following:

- How do middle school students fare in mathematics and science compared with their peers in other4 countries?
- What progress have middle school students made in the past three decades?
- What percentages of middle school students are currently achieving at the proficient level on NAEP?

- How do the achievement patterns of different socioeconomic, racial or ethnic, and gender subgroups compare with those of the general student population?[1]

Sources of Data and Limitations

We start with some international comparisons. For this, we relied on two sources: TIMSS, a cross-national survey of student achievement in mathematics and science among 9-, 13-, and 17-year-old students, and the four-year follow-up to this study (TIMSS-R). In describing the TIMSS and TIMSS-R findings, we specifically examine the differences in relative ranking of the cohort of students who were in 4th grade for the initial study and in 8th grade for TIMSS-R. We also refer to findings of the Programme International of Student Achievement (PISA), a survey of reading, mathematics, and science literacy administered to a sample of 15-year-olds in countries belonging to the Organization for Economic Cooperation and Development (OECD). The PISA findings have received a great deal of attention in Europe and hence are relevant as we attempt to assess the relative standing of middle-school-age students in the United States.

After the international comparisons, we review historical trends in achievement scores based on long-term trend data from NAEP, a nationwide survey of student achievement in a number of academic subjects administered to specific age groups (9-, 13-, and 17-year-olds) or to a specific grade level (4th, 8th, and 12th grades). We describe overall trends and compare achievement among students belonging to different gender and racial or ethnic groups. Second, in light of the current emphasis on accountability (including the NCLB legislation), we examine the percentages of students currently performing at the proficient level or higher on the NAEP reading, mathematics, and sciences assessments for different demographic groups.[2] We end the chapter with general conclusions that prioritize the challenges U.S. middle schools face. In light of these conclusions, we also make recommendations concerning how to address these challenges.

Readers should be aware that the limitations of available data sources circumscribe the kinds of interpretations that can be made about middle school achievement. Because of the sampling techniques that the data sources employed, none of the sources include 6th graders. Thus, our analysis of middle school achievement is

---

[1]In this chapter, the highest educational level either parent has obtained serves as the proxy for socioeconomic status. Although this does not directly measure economic status, previous studies have shown a strong relationship between parental education and socioeconomic status (Warburton et al., 2001).

[2]NAEP has several components, including the long-term trend NAEP and the main NAEP. The long-term trend NAEP is designed to track trends over time, and its content has not changed substantively since the assessment's inception. In contrast, the main NAEP is designed to be flexible enough to adapt to contemporary curricular reforms and changes in assessment approaches. Thus, results from the main NAEP and the long-term trend NAEP are not comparable and are considered to be different indicators of achievement.

restricted to the 7th and 8th grades. Additionally, the age-level sampling methods that TIMSS and long-term trend NAEP used limit the inferences that can be made about specific achievement at specific grade levels. Furthermore, although the majority of 13-year-olds are enrolled in 7th or 8th grade, some 13-year-olds are enrolled in other grades because of retention, accelerated advancement, or varying age of entry into the school system. Although the proportion of such students is likely to be small, it is nevertheless important to recognize that tests that use age-level sampling methods are not strictly measures of middle-grade achievement. Finally, although PISA's sampling scheme does not focus on middle school students, its findings reflect learning that occurred during the middle school years (that is, it provides an indication of the cumulative effects of schooling through the middle grades).

Although state assessments can provide additional information about middle school achievement, we do not focus on them because the results would be limited to the particular set of states chosen for analysis. Because the purpose of the chapter is to provide a picture of middle school achievement for the nation as a whole, we focus instead on findings from national and international sources.

Comparing U.S. Students with Their Peers in Other Countries

We used results from TIMSS and TIMSS-R to compare the performance of middle school students in mathematics and science with that of their international peers. To facilitate interpretation, we report only on the countries that had participating 4th graders in TIMSS and participating 8th graders in TIMSS-R. This allows an examination of the relative growth of the same cohort of students from 4th grade to 8th grade. The analyses for both mathematics and science include data from a total of 17 nations, representing a range of geographic locations and stages of economic development.[3]

Figure 4.1 shows the ranking of U.S. 4th and 8th graders relative to their peers in other countries in mathematics achievement. In the figure, the United States is denoted by a triangle, and other countries are denoted by circles. Figure 4.1 shows that, in mathematics, U.S. 4th grade students scored about at the international average, ranking ninth out of the 17 countries. By the 8th grade, however, the students were scoring significantly below the international average and were ranked above only five other nations.

---

[3]The 17 nations are Australia, Canada, Cyprus, the Czech Republic, England, Hong Kong, Hungary, Iran, Italy, Japan, Korea, Latvia, the Netherlands, New Zealand, Singapore, Slovenia, and the United States.

Figure 4.1
U.S. International Standing in Mathematics Achievement at 4th and 8th Grades, 1995 and 1999

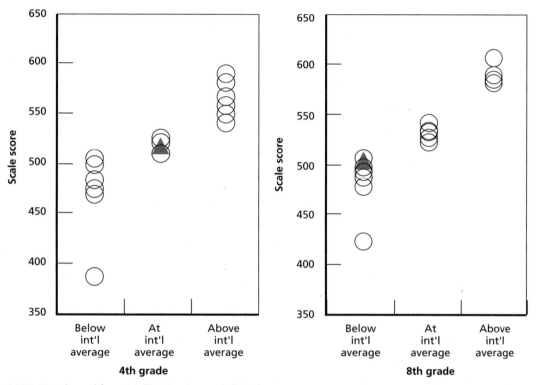

SOURCE: Adapted from Mullis, Martin, et al. (2000).
NOTES: Full scale is from 0 to 800. Triangles represent U.S. data; circles are other countries' data.
RAND *MG139-4.1*

Similar declines in performance were observed for science. Figure 4.2 shows the performance of U.S. 4th and 8th graders relative to that of their peers in other nations in science. Again, a triangle indicates the ranking of the United States, and circles indicate all other countries. In science, U.S. 4th graders scored significantly above the international average of the 17 nations, ranking third. As 8th graders, however, their relative performance declined. They were no longer performing above the international average and were ranked twelfth out of the 17 countries.

The findings suggest that U.S. children do not start out behind those of other nations in mathematics and science achievement, but they do lag by the end of the middle school years. The decline from 4th to 8th grade has elicited concern from some educators about the value of middle school instruction (Haycock and Ames, 2000), especially because a weak foundation in middle school could lead U.S. students to fall even further behind as they grow older. Indeed, international studies in

Figure 4.2
U.S. International Standing in Science Achievement at 4th and 8th Grades, 1995 and 1999

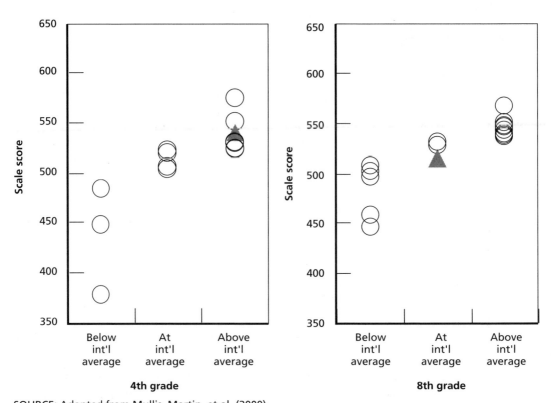

SOURCE: Adapted from Mullis, Martin, et al. (2000).
NOTES: Full scale is from 0 to 800. Triangles represent U.S. data; circles are other countries' data.
RAND *MG139-4.1*

mathematics and science conducted with 17-year-old students show that the relative performance of U.S. examinees is even worse at the secondary level than at the middle school level, with high school students scoring significantly below the international average in both mathematics and science (Mullis, Martin, et al., 1998).

Other surveys have confirmed that U.S. students do not fare well internationally, especially with respect to other wealthy nations. Using data from TIMSS and PISA, the United Nations Children's Fund (UNICEF) compared the academic performance of 13- and 15-year-olds across 14 OECD countries. The test scores were transformed into an "educational disadvantage" score indicating the proportion of students reaching and not reaching certain standards. In calculating the level of absolute educational disadvantage of each country, UNICEF noted that a large proportion of 13- and 15-year-olds in the United States fell below prespecified performance benchmarks on measures of reading, mathematics, and science achievement. Of

Figure 4.3
U.S. International Standing in Measures of Absolute Educational Disadvantage

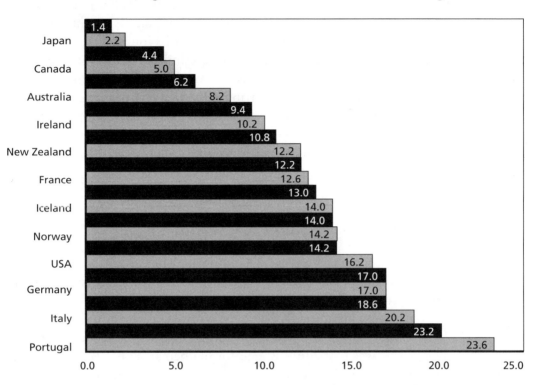

Average rank in five measures of absolute educational disadvantage

SOURCE: UNICEF (2000).
NOTE: A rank of 1 indicates a low level of educational disadvantage; a rank of 25 indicates a high level of educational disadvantage.
RAND *MG139-4.3*

the 24 nations, the United States was ranked 18th (see Figure 4.3). This led UNICEF (2002. p. 3) to conclude that

> a child starting school in Canada, Finland, or Korea, for example, has both a higher probability of reaching a given level of educational achievement and a lower probability of falling well below the average than a child starting school in Denmark, Germany, Greece, Hungary or the United States.

In sum, the international comparisons do not convey a favorable picture of the achievement of U.S. middle school age students. Although many of the other OECD countries may not have the disparity between the haves and have-nots or the same levels of racial or ethnic diversity as the United States, these factors alone cannot account for the standing of U.S. students. That 4th graders perform well on TIMSS but 8th graders do not suggests that economic conditions cannot explain differences in the relative performance levels for these two grades (Suter, 2000). Analyzing TIMSS results, Schmidt, Jakwerth, and McKnight (1998) found that the variability in student achievement levels in the United States is comparable to that in other countries. Furthermore, tabulations presented by Richard Houang (cited in Suter, 2000) showed that, even if all students belonging to ethnic or racial minorities are excluded, white U.S. students still rank in the lowest one-third of all countries at the end of secondary school. Thus, we cannot attribute the low relative rank of U.S students to the performance of specific racial or ethnic groups. However, differences between certain demographic groups should not be ignored; in later sections of this chapter, we therefore attempt to describe such group differences within the United States more fully.

Performance of Middle Grade Students Over Time

Monitoring changes in student achievement is important because it helps to determine how much progress has been made toward meeting educational goals and can inform future efforts to improve student achievement. In this section, we discuss changes in student achievement among 13-year-olds from the first administration of long-term NAEP in mathematics, science, and reading to the most recent administration in 1999. The NAEP was first administered for mathematics in 1978, for science in 1977, and for reading in 1971.[4] Results are presented for the nation as a whole, as well as for specific subgroups (gender and race or ethnicity). For a comprehensive discussion of long-term NAEP trends, see Campbell, Hombo, and Mazzeo (2000).

Nationwide Trends

Figure 4.4 compares the performance of today's middle school students with that of their 1970s predecessors. In mathematics, scores have generally been increasing since the mid-1980s, and students in 1999 scored significantly better than did students in 1978. Some educators have attributed these gains to investments in mathematics education that were prompted by the publication of *A Nation at Risk* in 1983 (National Commission on Excellence in Education, 1983), which portrayed the U.S. educational system as mediocre and in need of reform. Science education received a similar boost from the report, and middle school students in 1999 performed at a significantly higher level than did their 1977 counterparts. In reading, gains were observed between 1970 and 1980, but scores have since remained relatively steady. Despite the lack of progress in reading in recent years, 13-year-olds in 1999 nevertheless performed significantly better than did 13-year-olds in 1971.

---

[4]We do not provide results for extrapolated data in mathematics or science.

Figure 4.4
Average Scale Scores by Subject, 1971–1999

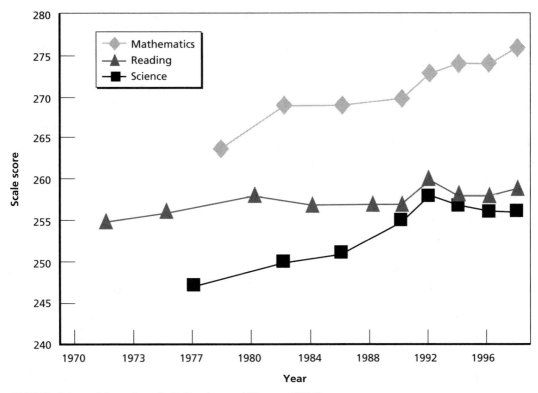

SOURCE: Adapted from Campbell, Hombo, and Mazzeo (2000).
NOTE: Scale is from 0 to 500.
RAND *MG139-4.4*

Trends Among Subgroups

Although overall historical trends are helpful for assessing the state of affairs in student achievement, it is also important to understand whether these trends hold true for different groups of students. To address this question, we examined score differences between males and females and between whites and ethnic minority groups (African-Americans and Latinos). Performance differences among these groups have attracted considerable attention, partly because the achievement gaps are believed to limit opportunities for higher education and future earnings (Carnevale, 1999). These concerns have given rise to numerous educational reform movements over the years that aim to improve equity in learning outcomes. In light of these concerted efforts, it is important to examine how achievement gaps between different groups of students have changed in the past three decades.

We present the results in effect sizes (the standardized mean differences) between two groups. If there were no group differences, the effect size would be 0.

Thus, the larger the effect, the greater the differences in mean performance. For the male-female analysis, positive values indicate that males have an advantage. For the white-minority analysis, positive values indicate that white students have an advantage. To guide interpretations of effect sizes, we followed the conventions set forth in Cohen (1988), which defines an effect size ranging from 0.20 to 0.49 as *small*, 0.50 to 0.79 as *medium*, and 0.80 or higher as *large*.

Trends Between Males and Females. Score differences between males and females exist in all three subject areas, but the direction and magnitude depend on the subject (see Figure 4.5). In mathematics, the advantage that females held during the late 1970s shifted toward males during the early 1980s. Since then, small average score differences in mathematics (the middle line) have favored males. Despite the fact that there was a change in the direction of the relative advantage, the gender gap in 1999 was not significantly different from that in 1978.

In science (the top line), score gaps favoring males have fluctuated somewhat throughout the assessment years, but gender differences in 1999 were comparable to

Figure 4.5
Average Scale Score Differences Between Males and Females by Subject, 1971–1999

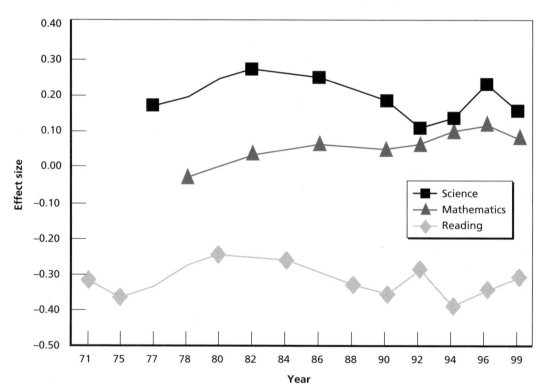

SOURCE: Campbell, Hombo, and Mazzeo (2000).
NOTE: Positive effect sizes indicate an advantage for males.
RAND MG139-4.5

those in 1977. Male-female score differences in reading (the bottom line) were larger than those in mathematics and science, but consistently favored females. As with the two other subject areas, the reading gender gap in 1999 was not significantly different from that observed in 1971. Overall, differences in test scores between males and females continue to exist, but the differences are considered small (all effect sizes are less than 0.50).

Trends Between Whites and Minorities.[5] Effect-size differences between African-American and white and between Latino and white examinees are shown in Figure 4.6. African-Americans have narrowed the gaps, with score differences in all three subject areas significantly smaller in 1999 than during the initial administrations. Despite this progress, however, white students, on average, continue to outperform African-American students by a substantial margin in all subjects, particularly in mathematics and science.

Figure 4.6
Average Scale Score Differences Between Whites and Minorities by Subject, 1971–1999

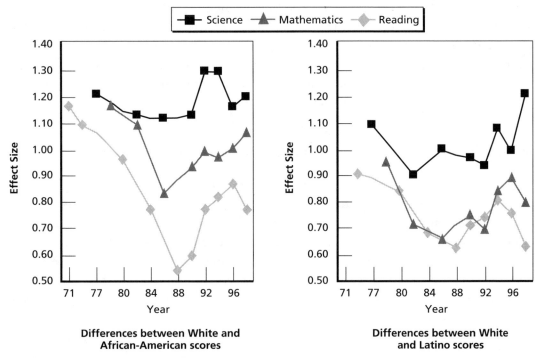

SOURCE: Campbell, Hombo, and Mazzeo (2000).
NOTE: Positive effect sizes indicate an advantage toward white examinees.
RAND *MG139-4.6*

_____

[5]The following discussion does not take socioeconomic factors into account. Racial and ethnic gaps within different socioeconomic levels will be discussed in another section.

Although differences in test scores between Latinos and white are not as large as the gaps between African-Americans and whites, they are nonetheless substantial—more than one standard deviation in some instances. Latino-white score differences have remained consistent in science: The score differences in 1999 were statistically comparable to those observed in the 1970s. Despite the apparent progress in reading, differences in Latino-white scores in 1999 were comparable to the score differences in 1975. In mathematics, however, the Latino-white score difference was smaller in 1999 than in 1978.

Summary of Nationwide and Subgroup Trends

Historical trends for students as a whole, as well as for particular subgroups, show a mixture of positive and negative results. On the encouraging side, the NAEP analyses of 13-year-old students between the 1970s and the late 1990s indicate overall improvements in mathematics, science, and reading, as well as declining achievement gaps between African-American and white students in all three subject areas. In addition to these positive findings, however, there were also findings that achievement differences in reading favoring girls and achievement differences in science favoring boys have not decreased since the 1970s. Similarly, the Latino-white achievement gaps in science and reading remain as large in 1999 as they were in the 1970s. Thus, efforts to reduce score differences have appeared to be effective in some cases (specifically, for African-Americans) but less effective in others (specifically, for Latinos in science and reading, for girls in science, and for boys in reading).

Achievement and the Accountability Movement

The TIMSS results indicating that the international standing of U.S. students declined from 4th to 8th grade and the NAEP results showing that some achievement gaps did not narrow have played a large role in strengthening today's "accountability" movement. The accountability movement establishes curricular or content standards that specify the skills and knowledge students must master to achieve high levels of academic competence. These standards are accompanied by assessments and various accountability provisions based on the results of the tests (Swanson and Stevenson, 2002).

The No Child Left Behind Act

Arguably the most prominent legislation relating to the accountability movement involves NCLB. NCLB mandates that states test all students annually in 3rd through 8th grades in mathematics and reading, and one year in the 10–12 grade span beginning in 2005. Science testing will be added in 2007, so that states will be evaluating science achievement annually in elementary, middle, and high school grades (specifically, in each of three grade spans: 3–5, 6–9, and 10–12).

A particular focus of NCLB is the performance of groups of students who have traditionally been disadvantaged. To ensure that all groups are making progress, states must report results disaggregated by race or ethnicity, socioeconomic status, English proficiency, and disability. Additionally, the act mandates that each group show a minimum threshold of gains each year. This ensures that overall trends of improvement in school or statewide averages are not masking poor or stagnant performances by particular subgroups.

NCLB also requires that states define performance standards for their assessments. Performance standards are definitions of what students should be able to do to reach particular achievement benchmarks, such as "basic," "proficient," or "advanced." In addition to requiring performance standards, NCLB mandates that all students attain the proficient level on their state assessments in mathematics and reading by 2013–2014. States are to reach this goal gradually, by defining performance objectives that specify the minimum level of improvement that school districts and schools must achieve each year. Schools that fail to make adequate yearly progress toward these thresholds can have sanctions imposed on them, including replacement of staff or reconstitution (restructuring of the school's governance arrangement by the state). Conversely, schools that exceed the performance goals can receive rewards, such as monetary bonuses or special designations.

Percentages of Middle-Grade Students Reaching Proficiency

Given the serious repercussions of not meeting the NCLB mandates, middle schools are facing unprecedented demands and pressures. An especially important concern for middle schools is whether they are in a position to meet the goal of having all students be "proficient" in 12 years. The following discussion addresses this issue by focusing on the percentages of students who are currently scoring at or above the proficient level on NAEP.[6] Although there are different interpretations of the term *proficient*, NAEP proficiency indicates a level of student achievement, derived from collective judgment of an expert panel, that represents full mastery of the knowledge and skills expected of students.

Because each state will be allowed to develop assessments according to its own content standards and to define *proficient* in its own way, the percentage of students reaching the proficient level on the state assessment will likely differ from the percentage reaching the proficient level on NAEP. Linn, Baker, and Betebenner (2002) showed that the state departments of education in Mississippi and Louisiana classified 39 percent and 7 percent, respectively, of their 8th grade students as proficient on their state mathematics assessments. In comparison, only 8 percent of Mississippi

---

[6]The NAEP performance standards have been criticized as being unreasonably stringent, and they may underestimate the percentage of students at or above a particular level (Shepard et al., 1993; Pellegrino, Jones, and Mitchell, 1999). Because the performance standards may be flawed, they should be viewed as developmental and interpreted with caution.

8th graders, but 12 percent of Louisiana 8th graders, reached at least the proficient level in mathematics on the 2000 administration of state NAEP (Braswell, et al., 2001).[7] Thus, differences in rigor, content standards, and performance standards between NAEP and the state assessments mean that we will not be able to anticipate how a individual state will fare in meeting the federal initiative. Nevertheless, the following discussion provides some indication of the current ability of middle school students to achieve the NCLB goals.

The following analysis relies on 8th-grade mathematics, science, and reading results from the most recent assessments available for the main NAEP tests at the time of our research,[8] specifically, the 2000 administration of the mathematics assessment (Braswell et al., 2001), the 2000 administration of the science assessment (O'Sullivan et al., 2003), and the 1998 administration of the reading assessment (Donahue et al., 1999). We present nationwide results, in addition to results for students broken down by gender, by race or ethnicity, and by the highest level of education attained by either of their parents (as a proxy for socioeconomic status).[9] For more information about the results of a particular assessment, see the NAEP Web site: http://nces.ed.gov/nationsreportcard/.

Nationwide. The majority of students nationwide failed to reach the proficient level, regardless of subject area tested. Approximately one-third of 8th graders nationwide attained proficiency in mathematics (27 percent), science (32 percent), and reading (33 percent). These statistics are sobering and lessen the optimism created by the improvements in achievement scores since the 1970s that were described in the previous section.

By Gender. In mathematics and science, slightly more males than females reached proficiency, whereas the reverse is true for reading. For males, 29 percent reached proficiency in mathematics, and 36 percent were proficient in science; for females, 25 percent were proficient in mathematics, and 27 percent were proficient in science. In reading, 40 percent of females attained the proficient level, compared with 27 percent of males.

By Race or Ethnicity. Very few Latino or African-American students reached the proficient level in any of the subject areas. For African-Americans, only 6 percent reached the proficient level in mathematics, 7 percent in science, and 12 percent in reading. For Latinos, 10 percent attained proficiency in mathematics; slighter higher percentages were observed in science (12 percent) and reading (15 percent). In con-

---

[7]Unlike main or long-term NAEP, state NAEP is designed to support state-level inferences. State NAEP assesses fourth- and eighth-grade students' skills in mathematics, reading, writing, and science. Until NCLB was passed into law, state NAEP was voluntary, with 42 states participating in the 2000 administration.

[8]Note that the results in this section use data from the main NAEP and therefore cannot be compared with the findings described in the previous section (which used long-term trend NAEP data).

[9]Although NCLB specifies that statewide achievement results be disaggregated by limited-English proficiency and disability status, NAEP does not currently provide results for these groups.

trast, significantly more whites were classified as proficient: 35 percent were proficient in mathematics, and 41 percent were proficient in science and reading. Thus, serious disparities exist between racial and ethnic groups in reaching set benchmarks.

By Level of Parental Education. Results for analyses using parental education as a proxy for socioeconomic status indicate that students from more privileged backgrounds (those whose parents have attained a higher level of education) are more likely to reach the proficient level than students whose parents received less schooling. In mathematics, 8 percent of students whose parents did not graduate from high school reached the proficient level, compared with 39 percent of students whose parents were college graduates. Similar patterns appeared for science and reading. In science, 44 percent of students with parents who graduated from college attained proficiency, compared with 8 percent of students whose parents had not finished high school. In reading, 45 percent of students with parents who were college graduates reached the proficient level, but only 11 percent of students with parents who did not graduate from high school did so. These statistics show that differences in socioeconomic status may compound previously indicated ethnic disparities. Hence, we next separately analyze each ethnic or racial group by parental education level.

Race or Ethnicity and Parental Education. Because NAEP reports do not tabulate results both by parental level of education and by race or ethnicity, we cannot report the percentage of students reaching proficiency for particular groups that may be of special interest (for example, minority students whose parents were college graduates). Therefore, we analyzed data from NELS:88 instead. NELS:88 uses a national probability sample to provide longitudinal data about critical educational experiences of students as they leave middle school and progress through high school and into postsecondary tracks. We used NELS:88 data to contrast the racial or ethnic gaps among students whose parents did not finish high school and students whose parents are college graduates. Specifically, within these two extreme levels of parental education, we examined the percentages of African-American, Latino, and white students reaching the maximum proficiency level on the NELS:88 mathematics, science, and reading tests.

We chose the maximum proficiency level on NELS:88 because it most resembled NAEP's "proficient" standard.[10] That is, the kinds of skills and knowledge needed to reach the maximum proficiency level on the NELS:88 achievement tests were similar to the kinds of skills and knowledge needed to reach the proficient level on NAEP. However, it is important to keep in mind that the NELS:88 maximum proficiency level is not directly comparable to the NAEP proficient standard.

Table 4.1 shows the percentages of students reaching the maximum proficiency level on the NELS:88 achievement tests, disaggregated by parental education and ethnicity. Regardless of race or ethnicity, students whose parents are college graduates

---

[10]Our analyses for other proficiency levels yielded similar interpretations.

are much more likely to reach the maximum proficiency level than students whose parents did not finish high school. However, racial or ethnic differences continue to persist among students whose parents have similar levels of attainment.

Differences are greater among students whose parents are well educated than among students whose parents have less education. For instance, among students whose parents did not finish high school, 5 percent of white students reached the maximum proficiency level, compared with 2 percent of African-American and 4 percent of Latino students. Among students whose parents are college graduates, 40 percent of white students reached the maximum proficiency level, compared with 16 percent of African-American and 24 percent of Latino students. Similar patterns were observed in science and reading.

Taken as a whole, these findings suggest that socioeconomic disadvantage does not entirely explain the differences in test performance between minority and white students and that other factors, including institutional racism, peer-group effects, and parental socialization, need to be examined as well.

In sum, the NAEP result suggests that few students are reaching the proficient level in mathematics, science, or reading. This is particularly true for minority students and for students whose parents did not finish high school. However, even among more-privileged students, such as those whose parents are college graduates, proficiency is difficult to attain: Over 50 percent of the students failed to reach the proficient standard in any of the core subject areas.

Understanding and Addressing Achievement Gaps

Achievement gaps between the haves and have-nots are one of the major challenges of U.S. education and not a unique problem that only middle schools face. On average, minority and low-income children start school less academically prepared than do white and higher-income youngsters (Lee and Burkam, 2002; Zill and West, 2001). This gap persists into elementary school, where nearly two-thirds of African-American and Latino children are two years below grade level in reading (Price,

Table 4.1
Percentages of Students Scoring at the Maximum Proficiency Level on NELS:88 by Parental Education, Ethnicity, and Subject

Group	Parents Did Not Finish High School			Parents Are College Graduates		
	Math	Reading	Science	Math	Reading	Science
Whites	5	19	10	40	56	42
African-Americans	2	9	8	16	29	20
Latinos	4	14	9	24	36	22

SOURCE: Carroll (2000).

2001) and where considerable socioeconomic status (SES) differences exist in reading and mathematics (Alexander and Entwisle, 1996). By the time students reach middle school, the achievement gaps are even more pronounced (Gross, 1993).

Many factors underlie the average achievement differences between poor and wealthy children. Research has shown, for example, that poor children (who are also disproportionately ethnic minorities) are more likely than wealthy children to have unqualified teachers, lack material resources, and be enrolled in larger classes (Stecher and Bohrnstedt, 2000). While these factors have been relatively well examined within the literature, a less-explored factor is differential rates of summer learning—the loss of learning during the summer months (Alexander and Entwisle, 1996). Consideration of learning opportunities during nonschool time is especially important in light of recent analyses of the positive effects of summer schools (Cooper, Nye, et al., 1996) and modified school calendars (Cooper, Valentine, et al., 2003) on the achievement of economically disadvantaged students. Although data on such programs are limited at this time, summer programs during the early grades of elementary school, when students are learning basic skills (and when the summer losses appear most substantial), might be particularly effective in helping to bridge the achievement gaps between different demographic groups (Cook, 1996). Whether such an early intervention can decrease the achievement gaps among student entering middle grades remains to be seen.

Challenges, Recommendations, and Exploratory Ideas

The picture of the achievement of 13-year-olds that NAEP statistics portray is more complex than is typically conveyed, and there are some positive trends. NAEP data suggest that there has been slight but steady progress during the past three decades. Today's middle school students are performing at a higher level in mathematics, science, and reading than did their counterparts in the 1970s. Achievement differences between African-Americans and whites have narrowed in all three subject areas since the early 1970s, as have achievement differences between Latinos and whites in mathematics. *These results suggest that the efforts made thus far to reduce performance gaps among some of the racial groups have been somewhat successful.*

Unfortunately, the reasons for the positive changes are not well understood. For example, although some gains have been made since the 1970s, we do not know whether middle school organizational and instructional practices (see Chapter Three) have or have not contributed to these gains in achievement.

But while the analyses of the NAEP scores show achievement gains, other indicators convey a bleaker picture of the performance of middle school students and help us identify some of the major challenges middle schools face today:

- International comparison studies show that the relative performance of U.S. students in mathematics and science declines from elementary school to middle school and that U.S. 13- and 15-year-olds are more likely to be educationally disadvantaged than their peers in other wealthy nations.
- Compared with the first administration of the NAEP, achievement gaps between Latinos and whites have generally persisted, as have male-female achievement differences.
- The majority of 8th graders fail to reach the proficient level in mathematics, reading, and science. This is particularly true for Latinos and African-Americans, who continue to lag behind their white counterparts, even when their parents have attained college education.

Among the challenges U.S. middle schools face today, raising achievement levels to meet the NCLB mandates clearly ranks high. If middle schools are to achieve the NCLB goals, significant changes must occur. It is particularly important to have additional resources directed toward the lowest-performing students, who disproportionately consist of ethnic minorities and poor children. Although past efforts have narrowed the achievement gaps, Latinos and African-Americans continue to trail white students, and students whose parents have a college degree continue to outperform students whose parents have not finished high school. *Bridging such gaps might require greater (and wiser) investments in state- or federally funded efforts to lessen the achievement gaps between advantaged and disadvantaged students.*

Indeed, NCLB has expanded the roles of state and federal governments in improving education. NCLB requires the U.S. Department of Education to provide technical assistance to state agencies which, in turn, must provide technical assistance to districts. Districts must then provide technical assistance to schools. Assistance can encompass a variety of services, from increasing the professional development infrastructure to offering supplemental educational services (for example, after-school programs, remedial classes, tutoring). At the moment, it is not known which forms of support provide the largest payoff. *With the goal of decreasing the disparities among students entering middle grades, we recommend evaluation of various forms of supplemental services for the lowest-performing students, including summer school programs before 6th grade.*

But low achievement is not a problem only for some demographic groups. As our review indicated, even among the most privileged students, over half fail to reach the set standards. There are a multitude of potential reasons that very low proportions of students reach proficient levels of achievement. For example, the curriculum content might not be well aligned with the standards; the quality of instruction might compromise the performance of students; or the standards might be unrealistically high. Regardless of the reasons, we cannot expect middle schools to raise student performance to a proficient level while shouldering the burden of poor prior preparation.

We propose that the responsibility for improving the performance of low-achieving students should not rest solely on middle schools. As mentioned earlier, elementary schools could implement programs targeted at improving the performance of low-achieving students to prepare them for the transition to middle school. Improved accountability is especially critical across school transitions.

CHAPTER FIVE

Conditions for Student Learning

The preceding chapter suggested that the middle school years are not marked by the large gains on standardized achievement tests that one might expect from the emerging reasoning abilities and improved cognitive processing that take place at this age (Keating, 1990). However, from the review of the research in Chapter Two, it should now be evident that we need to examine academic performance of young teens in relation to other indicators of their adjustment as they transition to middle schools.

This chapter focuses on students' social-emotional well-being, engagement, school context, and climate. We begin with a brief review of studies that examine the association between students' social-emotional well-being and their academic performance. We also discuss how academic disengagement and feelings of social alienation during middle school increase the risk of poor educational outcomes, including dropping out. In addition, we review research on school climate and the prevalence of disciplinary problems and their effects on academic performance. Highlighting school safety issues, we discuss how unsafe environments might affect student behavior and well-being. Focusing on student perceptions of the conditions for learning, we end this chapter with our analyses of international HBSC data from WHO. We compare different social-motivational indicators for middle-school-age U.S. students with their same-age peers in 11 other countries. These international analyses allow us to compare the school-related perceptions of young teens in the United States with those in other Western countries for the first time.

Among the questions this chapter addresses are the following:

- Are social-emotional well-being and academic performance related?
- What conditions enhance or detract from student learning?
- How do U.S. students' views of the conditions for learning compare with those of their peers in other countries?

Social-Emotional Problems and School Functioning

Recent epidemiological studies suggest that 12 to 30 percent of U.S. school-age children and youth experience at least moderate behavioral, social, or emotional problems (Hoagwood, 1995; Mrazek and Haggerty, 1994; Kazdin, 1993). Kessler, et al. (1995) estimate that mental health problems jeopardize educational attainment for about 7.2 million young Americans. Because many mental health problems (for example, anxiety among girls and conduct disorders among boys) increase around the same time that young teens are acclimating to middle school (Kazdin, 1993), it is particularly relevant to consider the effects of such problems on students' academic functioning during middle school. Here, we briefly review studies that pertain to psychological distress (for example, anxiety, depression), as well as those that pertain to conduct problems (such as aggression and disruptiveness).

Several studies have shown that there is a robust association between depressive symptoms and poor academic functioning (Cole, 1990; Nolen-Hoksema, Seligman, and Girgus, 1992). Although many of the studies examine the associations between psychological and academic functioning concurrently, the two sets of problems are also linked to one another over time. For example, in a large longitudinal study of 7th graders, Roeser, Eccles, and Sameroff (1998) report that symptoms of emotional distress in 7th grade were associated with lower grades on report cards by the end of 8th grade.

Similar to psychological distress, conduct problems are associated with poor academic performance (Aunola, Stattin, and Nurmi, 2000; Shann, 1999). Students who display behavioral problems are more likely to get lower grades (for example, Cairns and Cairns, 1994; Dryfoos, 1990) and to be placed in lower academic tracks (for example, Haskins, Walden, and Ramey, 1983; Kershaw, 1992). Behavioral problems can interfere with children's ability to concentrate on academics (or both types of problems may be explained by underlying problems, such as hyperactivity or impulsivity). It has been documented that earlier academic difficulties also predict subsequent problem behaviors, such as delinquency, drug abuse, and dropping out of school (Cairns and Cairns, 1994; Dryfoos, 1990; Roderick, 1993).

The association between problem behaviors and achievement also holds true at the school level. For example, Shann (1999) found that the lowest-achieving middle schools had the highest rates of antisocial behavior. In addition, Rutter et al. (1979) showed that, in England, the schools with more disciplinary problems are the same schools that have lower student achievement (success on examinations).

In sum, adaptive functioning across the psychosocial and academic domains is often linked (Masten and Coatsworth, 1998; Roeser, Eccles, and Sameroff, 1998). Given these findings, some researchers contend that students who display emotional distress or behavioral problems might not be ready to learn (Adelman, Taylor, and Schnieder, 1999). If this is the case, *attempts to improve achievement by focusing solely on academics may prove to be insufficient; there also is a need to address the social-emotional difficulties of young teens.* Alternatively, earlier academic problems may lead to subsequent adjustment difficulties, possibly reflecting either common underlying problems or lack of motivation associated with prolonged academic difficulties, as suggested below.

Disengagement, Social Alienation, and Dropping Out

In addition to social-emotional difficulties, motivational problems also relate to low achievement of middle school students. Lack of interest, negative attitudes toward school, social alienation, and disengagement are not only associated with poor grades but may also predict the ultimate school failure, dropping out.

Although dropping out typically takes place during high school, the process of disengagement and alienation that ultimately leads students to leave school prematurely may start as early as 1st grade but more often starts or is exacerbated during the middle school years (Alexander, Entwisle, and Kabanni, 2001; Ekstrom et al., 1986; Finn, 1989; Finn, 1993; Wehlage and Rutter, 1985). For example, Kaplan, Peck, and Kaplan (1997) documented that low grades in 7th grade predicted devaluing of grades by the 8th grade and that such attitudes directly increased the risk of dropping out. Furthermore, they found that, in addition to low grades, lack of motivation, relationships with deviant peers, and social alienation from school-based peer networks during grades 8 and 9 all independently contributed to the risk of dropping out among students in this large sample from the Houston Independent School District.

Guided by a life-course perspective, Alexander, Entwisle, and Kabanni (2001) demonstrated that poor school performance and disengagement behaviors starting in 1st grade increased the risk of dropping out for members of a high-risk sample in Baltimore. Controlling for school performance and for students' disengagement, they found the following:

- Repeating a grade during middle school increased the probability of dropping out sevenfold.
- Eighty percent of those who repeated a class more than once were likely to drop out.

Because these effects of grade retention were obtained over and beyond those accounted for by prior grades and disengagement, the authors concluded that standing out and not fitting in are especially detrimental during the middle school years. Hence, it seems that *while low grades predict grade retention, the negative social consequences of being held back among 12–15 year olds further increases the risk of dropping out.*

In sum, disengagement and social alienation, typically accompanied by a history of poor school performance and grade retention (especially during middle school), contribute to the risk of leaving school early, which is a costly societal problem (Finn, 1989; Finn, 1993; Wehlage and Rutter, 1985). For example, the earnings of dropouts lag behind those who have completed high school even when earnings are adjusted for differences in school achievement and other indicators that distinguish dropouts from graduates (Natriello, Pallas, and McDill, 1986). Furthermore, about half of welfare recipients (see Alexander, Entwisle, and Kabanni, 2001) and half of the prison population are high school dropouts (Educational Testing Service, 1995; National Research Council, 1993).

In light of the statistics on dropouts[1] and the research that depicts the processes that can explain the predictors of dropping out, the middle school years are critical. *Failed opportunities to engage youths in middle school may have life-long consequences.*

Classroom Context and School Climate

Classroom context (for example, the level of disruption) and school climate (for example, sense of support, connectedness) are factors that can either increase individual vulnerabilities or promote resiliency. These environmental factors appear to be especially critical for

- students who display early signs of academic or social-emotional problems
- students from economically disadvantaged families
- students who experience substantial changes in their school environment during the transition to middle school.

Students who display behavioral problems early on are at increased risk for subsequent problems when placed in certain types of classrooms. For example, Kellam et al. (1998) found that aggressive boys placed in 1st-grade classrooms that were highly disruptive were at the highest risk of being identified as the most aggressive students in middle school. When students are placed in classrooms with other misbehaving and low-performing students, both the behavioral and academic gaps tend to widen between groups of low and high ability (Grant, 1991; Kellam et al., 1998; Kershaw, 1992). Thus, the classroom environment (such elements as student composition, the ability of teachers to provide support and effectively deal with problem behavior) can either increase or decrease the later repercussions associated with early signs of trouble (see also Kuperminc, Leadbeater, and Blatt, 2001).

Student perceptions of supportive climate and sense of community, in turn, are generally related to positive outcomes, such as increased motivation and lower levels

---

[1]Recent analyses of CCD data by Bedard (2003) suggest that earlier transition (after 4th or 5th grade) is more costly and increases the likelihood of dropping out.

of problem behaviors among young teens (Battistich et al. 1997). Some scholars propose that a sense of connectedness and support at school might be particularly important for students from economically disadvantaged homes who might otherwise lack such support (Becker and Luthar, 2002; Pianta and Walsh, 1996; Weinstein, 2002). For example, Battistich et al. (1995) found that a sense of school as a community was associated with more-positive academic attitudes, especially among the most-disadvantaged students. However, highly caring schools for disadvantaged students that lack academic focus may be too forgiving and therefore do not promote achievement.[2]

Finally, research on middle school transitions shows that, although grades and engagement tend to decline after students transition to middle school, student perceptions of the school environment can buffer negative changes (Eccles, Midgley, et al., 1993; Roeser, Eccles, and Sameroff, 1998; Roeser, Eccles, and Freedman-Doan, 1999). For example, Midgley, Feldlaufer, and Eccles (1988) showed that, students whose perceptions of teacher support declined between elementary and middle school valued the school subject less, but those who viewed teacher support as having increased valued the subject more.

In sum, student characteristics and school and classroom environments interact in ways that either decrease or increase the risk of academic and adjustment problems during the middle grades. Although it has been shown that community climate and support alone are insufficient to promote achievement gains in the middle grades (Phillips, 1997), *a balance between perceived support and academic demands seems to promote both achievement and social-emotional well-being, and this balance is particularly important for certain groups of youth* (Lee and Smith, 1999; Lee et al., 1999; Midgley and Edelin, 1998).

School Safety

School safety is one particular school environmental factor that has received a great deal of public attention lately (Juvonen, 2002). Although many of the most violent school shooting incidents in the 1990s took place in high schools, national statistics reveal that middle schools are equally unsafe (or even less safe, depending on the indicator used). School-level statistics show that 74 percent of public middle schools (compared with 45 percent of public elementary schools and 77 percent of public high schools) reported one or more criminal incidents to police in 1996–1997. Physical fights without a weapon were the most common form of reported crime in

---

[2]Stevenson and Stigler (1992) found that almost half the teachers they studied in Chicago believed that "sensitivity to the needs and personality characteristics of individual children" is the most important attribute of good teaching, while fewer than 10 percent of their colleagues believed that "ability to explain things clearly" mattered the most (pp. 166–167).

middle schools based on the Principal/School Disciplinarian Survey of School Violence in 1997 (U.S. Department of Education, 1997).

In one stratified random sample of 1,000 middle school students in Maryland (St. George and Thomas, 1997), 20 percent of students reported engaging in fighting on a regular basis. In addition, 35 percent of the sample reported having fought in the past. The same surveys also showed that 7th-grade boys were most likely to report fighting at school in the past six months (7 percent of 7th-grade boys, as opposed to 2 to 5 percent of older males).

Based on the National Longitudinal Study of Adolescent Health (NLSAH) (Carolina Population Center, 1997), over 9 percent of 8th-grade and about 6 percent of 7th-grade males revealed that they carried a weapon to school in the past 30 days. Kingery, Coggeshall and Alford (1998) found that feelings of vulnerability (such as the perception that people do not look after one another) and social alienation (such as feeling distant from other people in their schools) increased the risk for weapon-carrying among 9th through 12th graders (data were not available on students in lower grades).

National surveys of school safety that rely on teacher reports show that middle and junior high school teachers were more likely than teachers at other grade levels to report experiencing nonfatal crimes at school, although not significantly more than high school teachers (Young, 2002). In our analyses of the SASS data (see Chapters Six and Seven), we found that 8 percent of middle school teachers (grades 5–8[3]) reported that a student had physically attacked them. This figure was higher for middle school teachers than for high school teachers (6 percent of high school teachers stated that a student had physically attacked them). Furthermore, 23 percent of middle school teachers surveyed reported having been threatened by a student in their current school. They reported an average of 2.7 threats from students within the past year. Little is known about the effects of incidents and threats on teacher dissatisfaction, distress, and turnover.

Although serious forms of violence are rare among students, middle school students are at highest risk of less physically serious harm. The latest school safety data (Young, 2002) indicate that 14 percent of 6th graders were bullied compared with 2 percent of 12th graders in 2001. Moreover, 22 percent of middle school youth reported having been threatened with a beating (Gottfredson et al., 2000).

Taken together, the school violence statistics document that middle school environments are less than optimal workplaces for both students and teachers. Thus, *school safety is one of the main challenges for the American middle school.*

---

[3]Consistent with other research on the middle grades, we broadly defined *middle* schools as including grades 5–8, 6–8, and 7–8; *elementary* schools as including grades K–5 and K–6; and *high* schools as including 9–12 and 10–12.

Safety Concerns and School Functioning

How do incidents and threats of harm inflicted by schoolmates affect students? Victimization experiences, including threats and witnessing of other students getting hurt, are related to emotional distress and strategies that are either harmful to the students themselves (skipping school) or to others (carrying a gun).

Several recent studies have found a strong association between victimization experiences and psychological distress. The vast majority of this research focuses on the more prevalent forms of hostility, such as bullying (Nansel et al., 2001). Students who are bullied by their schoolmates report elevated social anxiety, depression, and feelings of loneliness (see Juvonen and Graham, 2001). Feelings of distress associated with bullying experiences, in turn, predict compromised school functioning (lower grades and higher rates of absenteeism) among middle school students (Juvonen, Nishina, and Graham, 2001).

Unsafe schools affect not only those who personally experience harm but also those who witness such incidents. National Household Education Survey (NHES) data show that half of 6th- to 12th-grade students surveyed witnessed bullying, robbery, or physical assault at school in 1993 (Chandler, Nolin, and Davies, 1995). In 2001, 12- to 18-year-old students reported being more afraid of being attacked at school or on their way to and from school than away from school; 6th graders were most afraid of being attacked.

Earlier NHES analyses showed the following:

- Sixty percent of middle school students surveyed reported that they rely on some strategy to avoid harm at school.
- About 25 percent of middle or junior high school students reported that they deliberately stay away from certain places in the school to protect themselves.
- About 10 percent of African-American and Latino students in grades 6 through 12 (not reported separately for middle school) reported having stayed home from school because they were worried about being targeted.

The NCES report on these findings (Chandler, Nolin, and Davies, 1995, p. 3) concluded that

> Students who must think about avoiding harm at school are diverting energy that should be expended on learning. Improving students' safety at school will enable American youth to redirect their concerns to school work and student activities.

The findings regarding school safety, emotional distress, and school functioning are consistent with the most recent analyses on school climate. Brand et al. (2003) found that differences in student perceptions of safety problems accounted for about 30 percent of between school variance in both levels of depression and the academic aspirations of middle school students. Thus, school safety concerns affect not only individual students but the overall school climate and rates of problems that vary from school to school.

School Responses to Promote Safety

Schools are responding to safety problems and concerns in a variety of ways. One method involves identifying at-risk youth (for example, those displaying "warning signs" for violence) for special interventions (for example, for anger management). However, such targeted intervention programs can backfire. In a review of interventions for adolescent problem behavior, Lipsey (1992) reported that 29 percent of the studies examined were judged as harmful in that, unlike the behavior of their counterparts in control groups, intervention participants' problem behavior escalated. These effects can be at least partly accounted for by the social reinforcement or "deviancy training" that group members receive from one another for acting out (Dishion, McCord, and Poulin, 1999). Hence, creating separate programs for at risk youth may only exacerbate problems in the long run.

Another popular method of dealing with violent or hostile student behavior consists of "get tough" zero-tolerance policies. However, there is no evidence suggesting that these policies help students improve their behavior or that suspensions and expulsions prevent further disciplinary problems. In fact, evidence suggests that zero-tolerance policies increase student resentment and worsen school climate (Skiba and Peterson, 1999; Skiba, 2001). Recent findings of the NLSAH (McNeely, Nonnemaker, and Blum, 2002) also show that harsher disciplinary policies decrease feelings of school connectedness that are positively associated with better emotional well-being (Resnick et al., 1997).

In contrast to targeted interventions and zero-tolerance policies, schoolwide antibullying programs that aim to change the social norms of the school have been shown to decrease hostile incidents over time (Olweus, 1991); improve student psychological well-being; and reduce physical complaints, including headaches and stomachaches (Rigby, 2001). Such systemic schoolwide prevention programs require increased awareness of the nature of peer-directed hostilities and their negative effects, and school staff and fellow students must respond consistently to hostile incidents (Juvonen and Graham, in press). Hence, proactive efforts to change the peer culture of schools by raising the consciousness and social responsibility of the students may both decrease problem behavior and improve perceptions of support.

International Comparisons of Conditions for Learning

National statistics on social-emotional difficulties among young teens, disciplinary problems, and rates of victimization in middle school convey a troublesome picture, but little is known about how U.S. students and schools compare internationally. To gain a better understanding of whether the problems U.S. middle schools face are unique, we now turn to international comparisons of how students perceive their own well-being and social environments. WHO's HBSC survey allows us to compare U.S. middle grade students' perceptions to those of their peers in 11 other Western countries across a range of social-motivational indicators.

HBSC is an international survey administered to 11-, 13-, and 15-year-olds in different parts of Europe, in North America, and in Israel.[4] HSBC's objectives are to monitor trends in adolescents' behaviors and attitudes over time and to provide information about the contexts in which these attitudes and behaviors develop. The HBSC surveys for each nation contain a common set of items in four areas: background factors, individual and social resources, health behaviors (for example, drug use), and health outcomes (for example, somatic complaints).

In this section, we focus our analyses on school-related questions and indicators of student psychosocial adjustment among 11.5- to 14.5-year-old students, based on data collected in 1997 and 1998. We focus on this age group because that is when U.S. students are most likely to be in middle schools (grades 6–8). Our goals were to

- identify factors that describe conditions for learning (that is, students' perceptions about their school context and psychosocial well-being)
- examine how the perceptions of U.S. teens compare with those of their same-age peers in other Western nations.

We obtained school-relevant data from the HBSC survey for 12 countries that also have TIMSS-R achievement data. Although we cannot make direct comparisons between the TIMSS and HBSC, because the samples are not comparable (for example, 13-year-old students in TIMSS and 11.5- to 14.5-year-old students in HBSC), including data from both sources allows some rough estimates of *relative rankings* among the 12 countries across various indices of school functioning.[5] With the HBSC data, our goal was to rank the U.S. students on indicators that capture student perceptions of the conditions for learning.

There were pertinent data on 32,793 students (of the 56,237 total observations included in the international HBSC data set). We sampled approximately 2,000 to 4,000 students from each country and used weighting to ensure that our samples were representative of the samples within each country.

We used factor analysis to identify the underlying constructs that depict different aspects of students' perceptions of their school social context and their psychosocial adjustment. Appendix C describes the scale development, including the factor

---

[4]The target populations of the HBSC study are 11-, 13-, and 15-year-olds attending school. However, to achieve the sampling strategy of having the mean ages in each country be 11.5, 13.5, and 15.5, other age groups were sampled as well.

[5]Comparisons of TIMSS-R data for these 12 countries reveal that U.S. 8th graders rank among the bottom third of the group.

analysis methods and the psychometric properties of the scales that we used to compare the countries.

Through our factor-analytic and other scale-construction methods, we computed seven scales:

- *emotional and physical problems*
  - headaches
  - stomachaches
  - irritable mood-bad temper
  - feeling low
  - nervous
  - sleeping difficulties
- *school climate*
  - School is a nice place.
  - I belong at school.
  - School rules are fair.
  - I take part in setting rules.
  - I like school.
  - School is boring.
- *social isolation*
  - I feel left out of things.
  - I am alone at school.
  - I feel lonely, helpless.
  - I have been bullied.
- *peer culture*
  - Students enjoy being together.
  - Students are kind and helpful.
  - Students accept me.
- *teacher support*
  - Teachers encourage me to express my own view.
  - Teachers treat students fairly.
  - I get help from teachers when I need it.
  - Teachers are interested in me.
- *parental involvement*
  - My parents are ready to help.
  - My parents come to school.
  - My parents encourage me to do well.
- *perceived pressure*
  - Teachers expect too much.
  - Parents expect too much.

We were able to differentiate among various perceptions of the school environment that other studies might incorporate into more general indicators of school climate. These more-specific scales allowed us to make finer distinctions. For example, students might view the peer culture of their school as unkind but perceive their teachers as supportive, or they may feel socially isolated in school but view their parents as involved.

The scale scores depicted in the following figures are standardized within the whole sample. Thus, the international sample mean is 0 and the standard deviation is 1. Positive scores indicate values greater than the sample mean for this particular group of countries, and negative values indicate values lower than the sample mean. In each graph, the nations are listed according to their score on the particular factor depicted: Nations scoring favorably on the factor are at the top of the ranking; those scoring the worst are at the bottom.

Emotional and Physical Problems

As shown in Figure 5.1, the United States ranks lowest on this scale, which shows that U.S. students report the highest level of emotional and physical problems. The U.S. students reported more problems (more than 1.5 standard deviation above the sample mean), such as headaches and feeling low and nervous, than did their peers in all other nations except for Israel.

School Climate

Middle-school-age students in the United States fare the worst among their peers in all other Western nations on school climate. That is, U.S. teens do not consider their schools to be pleasant places where they feel they belong. Their ratings of school climate are almost two standard deviations below the 12-nation sample mean (illustrated in Figure 5.2).

Social Isolation

As shown in Figure 5.3, middle-school-age students in the United States report feeling more socially isolated (such as being left out, lonely, helpless, or bullied) than do their peers in eight other nations, but less so than in Latvia, Israel, and Lithuania. Although the U.S. mean score is "average" (that is, at about 0) for this group of 12 countries, the U.S. students are in the bottom quarter of the 12 nations on this measure of social isolation.

Peer Culture

Students in the United States report having less positive peer culture at school than do students in other nations, except for the Czech Republic. That is, the U.S. students report that their schoolmates are not kind, helpful and accepting and do not

Figure 5.1
Student-Reported Emotional and Physical Problems

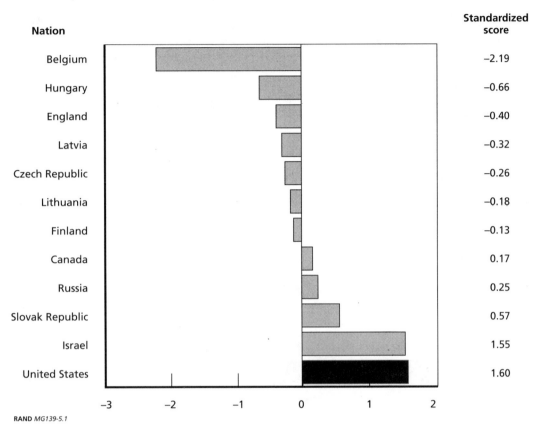

Nation	Standardized score
Belgium	–2.19
Hungary	–0.66
England	–0.40
Latvia	–0.32
Czech Republic	–0.26
Lithuania	–0.18
Finland	–0.13
Canada	0.17
Russia	0.25
Slovak Republic	0.57
Israel	1.55
United States	1.60

RAND *MG139-5.1*

enjoy one another's company. As shown in Figure 5.4, U.S. teens score more than one standard deviation below the international sample mean on this index of peer culture.

Teacher Support

As shown in Figure 5.5, U.S. middle-school-age students ranked sixth among the 12 countries on teacher support. This means that the U.S. students rated their teachers as more encouraging, fair, and supportive than did their peers in six other countries. U.S. students did not differ from their peers in England, Belgium, and Lithuania in their perceptions of teacher support.

Parental Involvement

As shown in Figure 5.6, U.S. middle-school-age students viewed their parents as being relatively involved (for example, that parents are helpful and encouraging and that they attend school events) compared with their peers in other countries. U.S.

Figure 5.2
Student-Reported School Climate

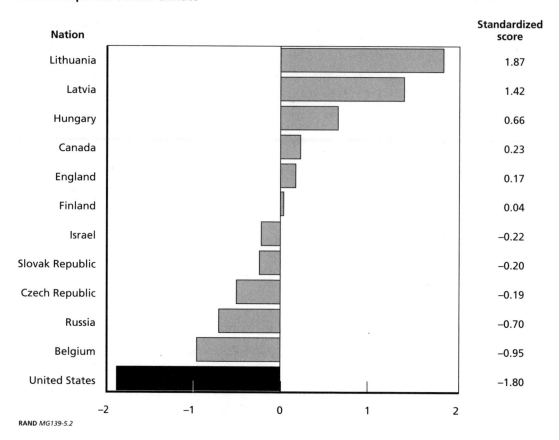

RAND MG139-5.2

student perceptions are not significantly different from those of their peers in Canada, Slovakia, Israel, and Hungary.

Perceived School Pressure

U.S. students feel less pressure from teachers and parents to do well in school than does the average student in the international sample (illustrated in Figure 5.7). There is no significant difference between the United States and Belgium, England, and the Czech Republic on this factor.

In addition to the country comparison, we conducted analyses by parental education level. Among the U.S. students, those whose parents did not finish high school consistently rated their learning conditions more negatively than did their peers from more highly educated families. At the same time, the U.S. students whose parents had completed higher levels of education still rated the conditions for learning more negatively than did their Canadian counterparts, for example. Thus, even U.S. students from highly educated families (some of whom attend private rather than public schools) do not reach the level of their international peers.

Figure 5.3
Student-Reported Social Isolation

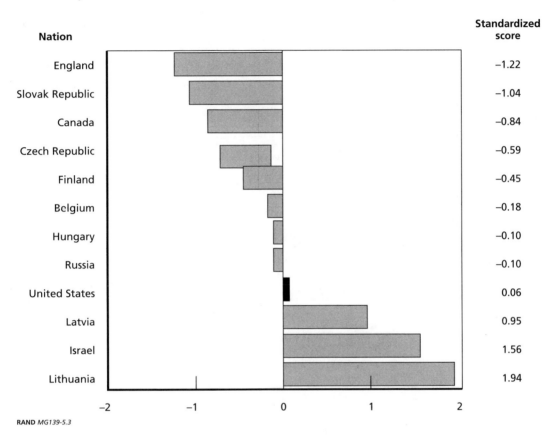

RAND MG139-5.3

In sum, *the international comparisons of the HBSC data show that U.S. middle-school-age students have negative perceptions of their learning conditions.* Compared with their peers in other countries, they

- report the highest levels of emotional and physical problems
- view the climate of their schools most negatively
- consider the peer culture in school to be unkind and unsupportive.

U.S. students rank within the top half of the 12 countries on teacher support, parental involvement, and lack of perceived pressure to do well in school. The recent debates within the United States have indeed focused more on the importance of teacher support, parental involvement, and "academic press" than on school climate, peer culture, or emotional and physical health. These HBSC data did not allow us to examine the association between achievement and the factors that we use here to depict the conditions for learning. We encourage such studies for the future.

Figure 5.4
Student-Reported Peer Culture

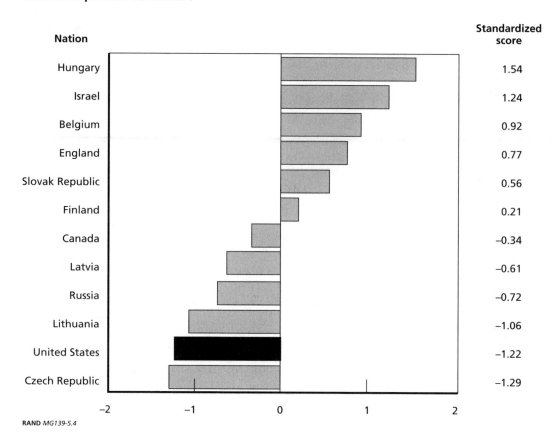

RAND MG139-5.4

Challenges, Recommendations, and Exploratory Ideas

In light of the current emphasis on school accountability and student achievement, we suspect that social-emotional well-being and feelings of connectedness will receive less and less attention. Yet research shows that *one of the challenges U.S. middle schools face is the relatively high number of students with social-emotional problems.* Because social-emotional problems are related to low academic performance, it is critical to understand the links between these problems to try to address them. Our literature review suggests that academic and social-emotional problems are related to one another in at least the following two ways:

- Early academic problems predict subsequent disengagement, as well as increased behavioral problems and dropping out.
- Feelings of anxiety and depression and concerns about personal safety in school can hinder learning.

Figure 5.5
Student-Reported Teacher Support

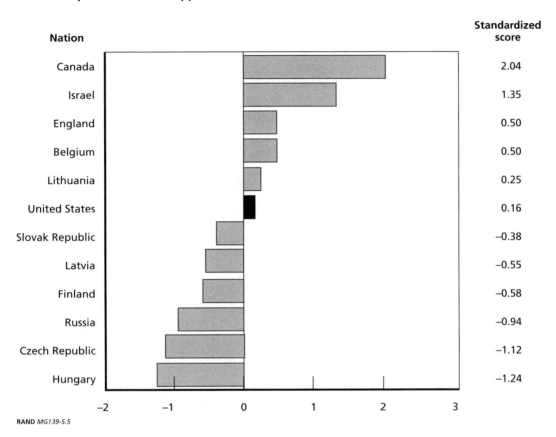

Nation	Standardized score
Canada	2.04
Israel	1.35
England	0.50
Belgium	0.50
Lithuania	0.25
United States	0.16
Slovak Republic	−0.38
Latvia	−0.55
Finland	−0.58
Russia	−0.94
Czech Republic	−1.12
Hungary	−1.24

RAND *MG139-5.5*

Failure to recognize the links between social-emotional, motivational, and academic problems may result in the use of well-intended educational practices that actually have negative long-term effects. For example, research shows that grade retention during middle school substantially increases the risk of dropping out and that the risk factors are not only academic (such as poor grades) but social. Hence, *we recommend that grade retention not be used to address academic problems during the middle grades but rather that alternative methods that do not compromise students' social adjustment be explored and used.*

Although many studies that examine the association between academic performance and social-motivational functioning focus on student risk factors, there is also a growing body of research demonstrating how classroom environment and school climate can increase either the vulnerabilities or the resiliency of students. *Particularly risky are middle school environments in which students feel disconnected from others, not supported or cared for, and unsafe.* In light of (a) the research documenting the links between social-emotional and academic problems, (b) the national statistics

Figure 5.6
Student-Reported Parental Involvement

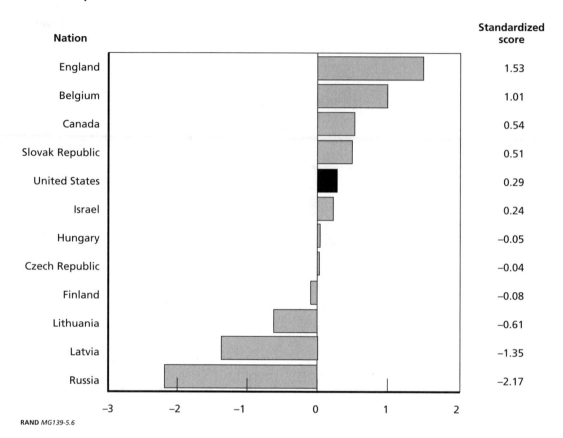

on middle school safety, and (c) our comparisons of international student perceptions of the conditions for learning, we conclude that improving the quality of learning conditions by preventing disciplinary problems and by fostering a caring school climate should be a high priority for U.S. middle schools.

Although school climate has been and continues to be a middle school reform goal (see Chapters Two and Nine), it appears that, in addition to such organizational strategies as teaming students in smaller units or including advisories, other changes that improve the quality of social interactions are needed. *We recommend that middle schools adopt comprehensive prevention models that focus on changing the social norms or the peer culture that fosters antisocial behavior.* To accomplish this, technical assistance and professional development that help middle school teachers and principals implement such programs are needed.

In light of our international comparisons, *we recommend further research and analysis of the reasons that student perceptions of their learning conditions are more posi-*

Figure 5.7
Student Perceptions of School Pressure

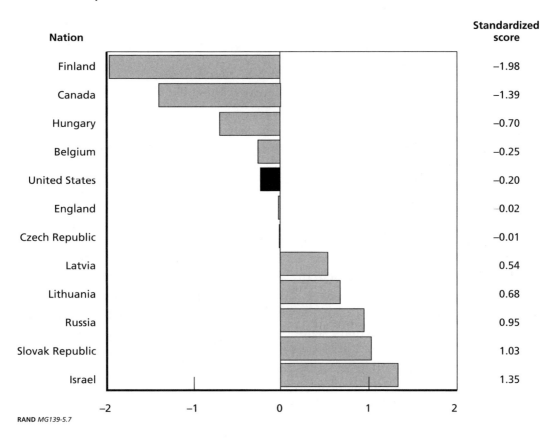

RAND *MG139-5.7*

tive in other countries. Such a program should gather information about how other countries educate their young teens, the structure and organizational characteristics of their schools, and their instructional practices. For example, why do Canadian students surpass their U.S. peers on achievement measures, consider their school climate more inviting, and believe their teachers and parents are more supportive? International comparisons were undertaken to study teaching practices after the well-publicized TIMSS findings. The U.S. Department of Education sponsored a TIMSS video study (Stigler and Hiebert, 1999) that specifically focused on examining the differences in instructional methods used in some key countries that outperform U.S. students. The information this study provided is now guiding educational reform through professional development that consists of facilitated teacher collaboration within an academic discipline (for example, math or science). We expect that similar efforts to better understand the school environments of different countries might eventually help us improve the conditions for learning in the United States as well.

CHAPTER SIX

Principals

As the organizational leaders of their schools, principals are in the position to foster school climate, thereby influencing both the learning conditions of students and the working conditions of teachers. Principals are also in the position to endorse and implement a particular reform or practice for their schools, establish procedures, prioritize goals for teachers and students, and monitor whether the procedures have been followed and the goals met.

Although principals have not been studied to the same extent as teachers or students, there is a growing body of research on school leadership, particularly because the increasing pressure to hold schools accountable for student performance (for example, from legislation, such as NCLB) places additional burdens on school administrators. In general, most of the research on principals does not distinguish among those who lead elementary schools, middle schools, and high schools. When studies make breakdowns by grade level, they typically compare elementary school principals with secondary school principals (combining middle and high schools in the secondary category) and pay little attention to how the circumstances or needs of middle school principals may differ. One exception is Valentine et al. (2002), a widely publicized source of information on middle school principals. However, the results of this study are not generalizable to the nation's middle schools because only 6.5 percent of the 14,107 middle school principals who were surveyed completed the entire survey instrument and only 10 percent of the respondents completed one section or more.

This chapter discusses the effects that principals have on schools and the various roles that they are supposed to perform. We also review and discuss the analyses we conducted using the SASS principal survey (SASS, 2001). To better understand how the challenges middle school principals face might differ from those of their elementary school and high school colleagues, we compared the responses across these three phases of schooling. Specifically, we examined what principals believe to be the problems in their schools, how they allocate their time, and how they prioritize their goals. Among the questions this chapter addresses are the following:

- What makes an effective principal?

- What roles must principals perform?
- How do middle school principals compare with their elementary and high school colleagues?

Effective Leadership

Researchers and experts have identified specific qualities or behaviors as being characteristic of successful school leaders. For example, the National Institute on Educational Governance, Finance, Policymaking, and Management (1999), a policy forum having a range of experts, including principals, teachers, researchers, and other stakeholders, considers the following to be among the qualities associated with good leadership:

- instructional leadership
- management skills
- vision
- communication
- collaboration
- community building.

The National Association for Elementary School Principals,[1] which is also the professional association for middle school principals, outlines similar standards for what principals should know and be able to do. According to this organization, principals should be able to

- balance management and leadership roles
- set high expectations and standards
- demand content and instruction that ensure student achievement
- create a culture of adult learning using multiple sources of data as diagnostic tools
- actively engage the community.

Empirical evidence supports the importance of these qualities for good leadership. For example, Teske and Schneider (1999) studied eight New York City schools with good reputations to identify characteristics of leadership at effective schools. Their findings were consistent with prior studies, including such qualities as leadership, vision, having a coherent education mission, and being able to control staff selection as important qualities of an effective principal. They also identified such qualities as entrepreneurship and setting high expectations as being important.

---

[1]This information was originally taken from the association's Web site at http://www.naesp.org/.

Research on school effectiveness has shed light on how principals might affect student achievement. Hallinger and Heck (1996) comprehensively reviewed the empirical research on this subject that had been published between 1980 and 1995. In seeking to understand the conceptual underpinnings of such research and the main findings, they identified several models for how principals influence student performance. Hallinger and Heck found little support for models suggesting that principals' actions affect student achievement directly. There was more support for mediated-effects models, which, unlike the direct-effects models, specify the processes of how principals affect student learning. Although there were some inconsistencies in these findings, one factor that emerged from the review is the importance of the principal having a vision and endorsing goals, especially academic ones.

But how do principals' visions and goals affect student achievement? Analyzing data from the HS&B data, Brewer (1993) found that high school principals influence student achievement by hiring teachers whose philosophies and practices are consistent with the principal's own goals and leadership style. So, the mere existence of goals is not likely to affect students unless principals can act in ways that promote their goals. Of course, myriad rules and regulations often restrict the ability of principals to promote their own goals (Chubb and Moe, 1990). How principals manage to prioritize goals and juggle multiple and, at times, competing goals is not well understood. However, research on school reform (Berends, Bodilly, and Kirby, 2002) may provide some insights into this question, inasmuch as principals in schools undergoing reform should, by definition, have a vision and should focus specifically on instructional goals even as they attend to routine tasks and follow regulations.

Principals' Perceptions of School Problems, Tasks, and Goals

To show whether the goals middle school principals endorse and the multiple demands they face are different from those of elementary or high school principals, we profile here results from our analyses of the latest SASS principal survey (SASS, 2001). SASS is a large-scale survey of a nationally representative sample of principals conducted by the U.S. Department of Education's NCES. Although NCES has surveyed both public and private school principals across multiple years, we describe only data for public school principals and focus on the 1999–2000 survey.[2] The SASS principal survey covers a wide range of topics, such as principals' perceptions of problems their schools face, time allocation, and goal setting and included responses from 8,524 principals. The surveys are linked to school information, enabling us to compare principals at schools of different levels.[3]

---

[2]See Fiore and Curtain (1997) for a detailed analysis of the 1987–1988, 1990–1991, and 1993–1994 surveys.

[3]Chapters Seven and Eight will present results from the teacher and school surveys, respectively.

We compared the responses of middle school principals to those of elementary and high school principals to find out how their perceptions of the most serious problems for their schools might differ, how they divide their time across different tasks, and what goals they regard as most important. To be consistent with other research on middle grades (such as McEwin, Dickinson, and Swaim, 1996), we defined *middle* schools as including grades 5–8, 6–8, and 7–8; *elementary* schools as including grades K–5 and K–6; and *high* schools as including 9–12 and 10–12.

Perceptions of Problems Schools Face

We examined what principals consider to be problems in their schools. On the SASS survey, principals were asked to rate the extent to which each issue was a problem at their school (on a scale of 1 to 4, with 4 being a serious problem, 3 a moderate problem, 2 a minor problem, and 1 not a problem). Although there were some statistically significant differences among principals across elementary, middle, and high schools,[4] all were small. To get a better sense of what these data meant, we ranked the perceived problems within each school level.

Table 6.1 shows that there are considerable similarities across the three levels in how principals perceived the problems their schools face. For example, the two top-rated problems are the same for all principals: unprepared students and a lack of parental involvement. Both middle and elementary school leaders also consider poverty to be among the top three problems facing their schools. Middle school principals differ from their elementary school and high school colleagues by ranking student apathy and disrespect for teachers as bigger problems facing their schools. These findings are consistent with those on motivation and disciplinary problems that we reviewed in Chapters Two and Five.

Table 6.1
How Principals Ranked the Problems Their Schools Face

Problem	Elementary	Middle	High
Students unprepared	2	1	2
Poverty	1	2	5
Lack of parental involvement	3	3	1
Student apathy	10	4	6
Disrespect for teachers	7–8	5	7
Student tardiness	4	6	3
Student absenteeism	5	7	4
Physical conflict among students	7–8	8	9
Teacher absenteeism	9	9	8
Poor health of students	6	10	10

---

[4]For example, middle school principals rated physical conflict as being more of a problem than either elementary or high school principals did.

Time Allocation Across Tasks

Time allocation across tasks provides some insights into the priorities and demands of middle school principals. Based on the responses of the SASS survey, Table 6.2 illustrates the principals' responses when they were asked about how often they had engaged in various activities during the past month.

Across all three levels of schooling, principals reported that they engage in tasks related to maintaining the physical security of students, faculty, and other staff and managing school facilities, resources, and procedures (for example, maintenance, budget, schedule) almost every day. Instructional goals (for example, facilitating student learning and guiding development and evaluation of curriculum and instruction) received less frequent attention from all principals. Although there were statistically significant differences among principals across the three levels of schooling, all were small. Thus, based on these data, it appears that time allocation by principals across all three levels of schooling is more similar than different.

The middle school principals that the National Association of Secondary School Principals surveyed also reported on how they spend their time (Valentine et al., 2002). Although the survey's low response rate means that the sample may not be representative, these data complement our findings. Table 6.3 ranks how much time middle school principals reported spending on various tasks during a typical work week, juxtaposed with a ranking of how they think they should be spending their time. How they spend their time differs dramatically from how they think they should be spending it. The most striking differences pertain to school management (principals reported that they spent most of their time on management but ranked it as fourth in importance) and program development (principals ranked it as first in importance, but fifth in terms of actual time allocation).

Table 6.2
Principals' Monthly Time Allocation of Tasks

	Elementary	Middle	High
Maintain physical security	3.8	3.8	3.8
Manage facilities, resources, procedures	3.8	3.8	3.8
Supervise and evaluate faculty and staff	3.3	3.4	3.3
Facilitate student learning	3.4	3.4	3.2
Develop public relations	3.3	3.2	3.1
Build professional community	3.1	3.1	3.0
Facilitate achievement of school mission	3.2	3.1	3.0
Guide development and evaluation of curriculum and instruction	3.0	2.9	2.8
Attend district-level meetings	2.7	2.7	2.7
Provide professional development activities	2.5	2.4	2.4

NOTES: Response scale: 1 = never; 2 = once or twice a month; 3 = once or twice a week; 4 = every day.

Table 6.3
How Principals Ranked Their Weekly
Allocation of Time

	Do Spend	Should Spend
School management	1	4
Personnel	2	2
Student activities	3	6
Student behavior	4	8
Program development	5	1
Planning	6	3
District office	7	9
Community	8	7
Professional development	9	5

SOURCE: Valentine et al. (2002), p. 61.

In a study conducted for the Wallace–Reader's Digest Funds (Farkas, Johnson, et al., 2001), the polling firm Public Agenda asked public school principals how they spent their time in terms of being able to devote the appropriate amount of time to a range of issues.[5] For each of ten issues, respondents indicated whether the issues received more attention or less attention than they deserve or about the right amount of attention. Students with discipline problems and parents with complaints or special interests were ranked first and second in terms of getting more attention than they deserve (at 47 percent and 45 percent, respectively). At the other end of the spectrum, principals reported that teacher quality and training and conferences and professional meetings get less attention than they deserve (at 36 percent and 28 percent, respectively).

In sum, principals are responsible for many aspects of running schools, from overseeing day-to-day operations and meeting basic safety requirements to shaping the educational philosophy and setting expectations for learning. The analysis above suggests that middle school principals think that their time allocation is not ideal, considering the discrepancy between what they do and how they report that they would *like* to spend their time. Little is known about how principals make choices during the day-to-day operations of their schools. This topic would benefit from further research.

Principals' Goals

In the SASS survey, principals were asked about their professional goals and the extent to which their schools had reached various academic, organizational, and financial goals.

---

[5]The methodology section in the survey report did not specify the grade level of the schools at which the respondents were principals.

Principals were asked to rate their three most important goals from a list of eight options. In light of our review regarding the importance of academic goals, their own ratings of the worst problems affecting their schools, and their time allocations, we were interested in learning whether any of these issues would be reflected in the principals' goal setting.

Table 6.4 shows the frequency with which principals rated various goals as being among the three most important. There was considerable consensus among all principals about which goals are the most important and which goals are the least important. Encouragement of academic excellence, building of basic literacy, and promotion of good work habits were important for most principals. In contrast, promotion of specific moral values and promotion of multicultural awareness and understanding were top priorities only for a minority of principals at all three levels.

Middle school principals stood out regarding only one priority. More middle school principals (37 percent) than elementary school (30 percent) and high school (28 percent) principals considered promotion of personal growth among the three top goals.

Principals were also asked to indicate how far along their own *schools* were in reaching several goals related to the education program, organization or governance, finances, attracting and retaining students, student assessment, and parental involvement. In general, there was little difference across all these domains. On a scale of 1 (just beginning) to 4 (we have reached our goal), the range was from a low of 2.75 (involving parents in the school) to a high of 3.32 (attracting and retaining students). Middle school principals reported not being as far along as their elementary school colleagues in terms of implementing educational goals and involving parents in the school. However, they reported being farther along than high school principals in attracting and retaining students, developing a student assessment system, and involving parents in the school. The findings on parental involvement are consistent with our review of the literature on declining involvement across grade levels in Chapter Eight.

The survey also asked the principals whether they had met the performance goals that their districts or states had set for them. Of the middle school principals, 65 percent reported having met such goals. However, few schools received any type of reward or recognition for having done so. Among those that did, these took the form of

- nonmonetary recognition
- cash bonuses or resources for the entire school
- cash bonuses or resources for teachers.

On the other hand, of the remaining 35 percent of principals who reported that their school did not meet the district or state performance goals, the majority (77

Table 6.4
Principals' Ratings of Goals as Among Their Top Three Goals

	Elementary (%)	Middle (%)	High (%)
Encouraging academic excellence	69.3	73.8	75.0
Building basic literacy	87.0	71.7	64.4
Promoting good work habits and self-discipline	61.4	60.0	58.5
Promoting personal growth	30.3	37.4	27.9
Promoting human relations skills	26.3	26.5	23.1
Promoting multicultural awareness or understanding	11.5	14.0	11.2
Promoting occupational or vocational skills	6.2	8.6	31.8
Promoting specific moral values	8.0	8.1	8.0

percent) reported that they were required to write an improvement plan.[6] Slightly fewer than half were put on an evaluation cycle with target improvement dates, provided with additional resources to support instructional improvement, or provided with technical assistance from outside experts. Almost no schools reported facing more punitive kinds of discipline, such as being subject to reconstitution or takeover regulations, being required to replace the principal, or being penalized by a reduction in state or district funding.

These findings indicate that, during the 1999–2000 school year, no big benefits or costs appeared to be associated with meeting or not meeting state or district goals. Schools that did not meet the goals also did not receive any assistance for their improvements. Similar survey questions today would likely generate a different set of responses, as the passage of NCLB mandates that the consequences for schools that do not meet performance targets be more direct and comprehensive.

Challenges, Recommendations, and Exploratory Ideas

The results of the SASS principal survey supplement what we know from prior research on school leadership, particularly as they provide insight into the middle school principal, who is generally ignored in the broader literature. That said, middle school principals appear to be more like than different from their elementary and high school colleagues. Middle school leaders, like other principals, rank academic excellence as their top goal. However, there is little information about how they translate this goal into action and whether they manage to prioritize this goal over some other demands that might require more-immediate attention, such as a need to deal with physical conflict. Insights from research on school reform might be useful for helping administrators deal with multiple demands and prioritize tasks.

The overall message from our review suggests that *middle school principals appear to be facing a dilemma: balancing their goals against the tasks and responsibilities that*

---

[6]These frequencies are lower than what would be expected, given federal legislation in force at the time.

dominate their time.[7] Although this dilemma is not unique to middle schools, it is nevertheless a challenge that should be recognized and addressed. Even though the school effectiveness literature identifies the importance of instructional leadership, middle school principals appear to be spending considerable time on managing facilities and resources and on maintaining the physical security of the school and students. Clearly, we need to know more about *why* principals are not able to allocate their time in the ways they say they would prefer and how they make choices. *In-depth investigations of effective administrators would provide important insights into how these administrators prioritize and delegate tasks and how they manage their time.*

In small schools, it is possible to meet the multiple demands of being an effective instructional leader (such as having clear goals, being a visionary, and being a good communicator) and being an effective operational manager. But in large schools, it may be necessary to delegate some of the managerial activities. Yet, there is little empirical evidence or even discussion about fitting different management models to different school sizes and types.

Another topic that is absent from the general leadership research and from the middle school reform literature is the challenge of addressing student motivational and disciplinary problems. Middle school principals rated physical conflict as being more of a problem and ranked student apathy and disrespect for teachers as bigger problems than did their colleagues in elementary and high schools. These findings underscore the research findings reviewed in Chapter Five. *Student motivational and disciplinary problems are one of the major challenges middle schools and their principals face.*

Chapter Five refers to prevention programs that show promise for decreasing aggression and improving both school safety and the well-being of students. To ensure that these programs are appropriately implemented, *we recommend that middle school principals receive additional training on how to reduce disciplinary problems proactively and facilitate a school climate conducive to learning.* Middle school principals are also likely to benefit from on-the-job technical assistance in implementing practices and programs for fostering an improved school climate.

In sum, the methods and actions that effective middle school principals use to promote academic goals are critical but are not well understood. We know little about middle school principals in general and even less about their effectiveness or what makes some principals more successful than others in juggling the multiple demands placed upon them. This topic should be a high-priority research question for future study.

---

[7]That the survey did not ask about the specific kinds of issues identified in the literature could, however, be influencing this interpretation.

CHAPTER SEVEN

Promoting Teacher Competence Through Training

Many middle school advocates believe that improving education for middle school students hinges on improving the competence of teachers (Mizell, 2002; Cooney and Bottoms, 2003). Teacher capacity can be improved through the training teachers receive *before* they begin teaching (known as *preservice training*) and the training they receive on an ongoing basis *after* they begin teaching (known as *in-service training* or *professional development*). Among the questions this chapter addresses are the following:

- How are middle school teachers trained?
- How important is it that teachers have training specific to the subject they teach?
- How can professional development compensate when teacher preparation is lacking?

The chapter begins with a brief description of the preservice training for middle school teachers and continues with the perceived problems of the current certification structure. We next review recent research on professional development and discuss our analyses of the 1999–2000 SASS.[1] The chapter concludes with some recommendations and some suggestions for further research.

Preservice Training for Middle School Teachers

Unlike elementary and high school teachers, middle school teachers typically have not been trained to teach at the grade level they are teaching; rather, most have been trained to teach at either the elementary or the high school level. Middle school teachers certified at the elementary level may lack an in-depth knowledge of their subject area. Middle school teachers that were certified at the elementary or high school level may not understand the developmental needs of young adolescents or the

---

[1] We chose to examine data only on teachers in public schools, specifically excluding teachers in private, charter, and Bureau of Indian Affairs schools.

instructional practices advocated for today's middle schools. Thus, there is a push to require middle school teachers to obtain specific certification.

There are approximately 1,300 teacher-preparation programs in the United States. Although there is little information about these programs (Wilson, Floden, and Ferrini-Mundy, 2001), many of them do not offer specialized training for prospective middle school teachers. In the 1995–1996 school year, half of the nation's teacher-preparation institutions reported offering a specialized middle-level curriculum, ranging from specializations to courses and field experiences (McEwin, Dickinson, and Swaim, 1996). During that same school year, less than 25 percent of middle school teachers reported having specialized middle-level professional preparation (McEwin, Dickinson, and Swaim, 1996). In a recent survey of selected southern states, only 12 percent of middle school teachers reported having middle school certification (Flowers, Mertens, and Mulhall, 2002).

Whether a teacher receives specific training to teach at the middle school level depends to a great degree on whether the state one teaches in requires a middle school–specific certification or license. In 1997, 88 percent of all institutions with specialized middle school–preparation programs or courses were in states with specific middle school licensing or endorsement requirements. Currently, 44 states offer a middle level–specific certification; however, only 21 of these states require teachers to earn such a license or endorsement to be able to teach at this level (Gaskill, 2002).

Most teachers who do not have a middle school certification have an elementary certification. Teachers who are trained to teach at the elementary level are not required, typically, to master any given subject to the degree necessary to teach a it at the middle school level. Policymakers and researchers agree that teachers should have undergraduate or graduate coursework in the fields they teach, although opinions differ over how much coursework a teacher needs to complete (Young, 2002; Wilson, Floden, and Ferrini-Mundy, 2001).

Lack of Subject-Matter Expertise

Compared to the high school level, many middle school teachers of mathematics, science, and social studies are teaching out of their areas of preparation (Ingersoll, 1999). A recent NCES study (Young, 2002) reveals that approximately *44 percent of all middle school students and more than half of students in high-poverty middle schools take a class with a teacher who has not acquired at least a minor in the subject taught* (see "To Close the Gap, Quality Counts," 2003).

Most of the research on subject-matter-specific training has focused on mathematics. One study concluded that having a teacher with a major in mathematics improves the achievement of 8th-grade students but not that of 4th-grade students (Heaviside et al., 1998). Chaney (1995) found that strong subject-matter preparation of teachers in mathematics and science (and an undergraduate or graduate degree for mathematics or advanced courses for science) was related to improved student achievement. The ability to teach mathematics well may be particularly important at the middle school level. Students who learn algebra in 8th grade are more likely to apply to a four-year college, for example (Atanda, 1999). In general, research evidence suggests that students learning from teachers with preparation in a specific subject perform better on tests in that subject (Wilson, Floden, Ferrini-Mundy, 2001).

Researchers who have reviewed the evidence on subject-matter training believe that students in teacher training programs should be taught not only the content but also its conceptual underpinnings and a strong reasoning ability (Wilson, Floden, and Ferrini-Mundy, 2001). Other evidence, although not derived from research on middle schools, suggests that the effects of teachers' subject-matter preparation on student performance may be cumulative (Monk and King, 1994) and may be most apparent with courses of greater difficulty (Hawk, Coble, and Swanson, 1985). It is important not only that teachers possess subject-matter expertise but also that they know how to transmit this knowledge to students (Killion, 1999).

As Table 7.1 shows, at the middle school level (classified as grades 5–8 in this study[2]), between 11 percent and 22 percent of students enrolled in English, math, science, foreign language, social science, and the subfield history were in classes led by teachers without a major, minor, or certification in the subject taught during the school year 1999–2000 (Young, 2002). Between 29 percent and 40 percent of middle school students enrolled in biology or life science, physical science, or English as a second language or bilingual education classes had teachers who lacked a major, minor, or certification in the subject taught. As Table 7.1 shows, there was little change between the 1987–1988 and 1999–2000 school years in the percentages of middle school teachers lacking credentials in any subjects other than physical or health education. During both periods, a *middle* school student was much more likely to have a qualified gym teacher than a trained math teacher.

Not surprisingly, fewer teachers had certification and an in-field major at the middle school level than at the high school level in English; mathematics; science, including the subfields of biology, life science, and physical science; and social science over the 13-year period.

The problem of middle school teachers lacking subject-matter training is being addressed. The U.S. Department of Education recently released guidelines to interpret NCLB that stipulate that all teachers in Title I schools be qualified in core academic subjects by 2005. The recent guidance stresses that middle school teachers

---

[2]We realize that it is common for 5th-grade teachers to teach multiple subjects.

Table 7.1
Percentage of Students Taught by a Teacher Without a Minor, Major, or Certification in the Subject

Subject	1987–1988	1999–2000
English	19.5	17.4
Foreign language	NA[a]	13.8
Mathematics	17.2	21.9
Science	16.3	14.2
Biology or life science	32.9	28.8
Physical science	43.0	40.5
Social science	12.7	13.5
History	15.2	11.5
English as a second language or bilingual education	41.2	36.1
Arts and music	2.0	2.5
Physical education	5.8	3.4

[a]Not available.

must show mastery of any subject they teach.[3] New middle school teachers should have a bachelor's degree and have either (1) passed a rigorous state test in the subject matter they teach; (2) completed an academic major or graduate coursework equivalent to an academic major in each of the academic subjects they teach; or (3) have advanced certification or credentials. *New middle school teachers are subject to the same subject-matter knowledge requirements as are high school teachers.* Current middle school teachers will need to be evaluated to determine their subject-matter competency.

Educators and researchers debate another question related to subject-matter expertise: whether in-depth knowledge about the subject matter (for example, a major or minor in mathematics) alone is sufficient or whether more attention should be paid to the subject-matter pedagogy (for example, how to teach math). These issues are timely in the context of the new NCLB requirement that middle school teachers in Title I schools demonstrate core subject-matter expertise by 2005.

Lack of Training in Development of Young Teens

Middle school advocates want specialized training not just for subject-matter but also for specific instruction in teaching young adolescents. Many middle school researchers and advocates (for example, Jackson and Davis, 2000; McEwin and Dickinson, 1997; Cooney, 1998) believe that middle school teachers should have specialized training. A recent Carnegie report on middle schools (Jackson and Davis, 2000. p. 96) stipulated that specialized teacher preparation should instill the following in prospective teachers:

- a strong grasp of subject matter and the use of assessments

---

[3]The second draft of the guidelines is now online at http://www.ed.gov/programs/teacherqual/guidance.doc (as of December 3, 2003). See also: *Education Daily*, Vol. 35, No. 242, December 24, 2002; George (2002); and Brown (2002).

- pedagogical knowledge and skills grounded in an understanding of human development and learning theories
- an understanding of interdisciplinary teaming
- an understanding of young adolescents' developmental characteristics and needs
- an understanding of a school's governance system
- skills to support a safe and healthy school environment
- the capacity to engage parents and community members.

It is arguable that the only aspects of this training that are unique to the middle school years are the understanding of young adolescents and the focus on interdisciplinary teaming. The latter is not necessarily unique to middle schools but is advocated for and discussed by middle school constituents more often than others. Advocates believe that until more teacher-preparation programs provide quality training on teaching in middle school, they will continue to turn out teachers who are unfamiliar with effective approaches to promoting young adolescents' social, emotional, physical, and intellectual growth (Lipsitz, Jackson, and Austin, 1997). However, given the current literature, it is unclear whether specialized training will help teachers apply their developmental knowledge to specific classroom management methods or instructional approaches.

There is some evidence to suggest that middle school teachers who have been trained to teach at this level value their preparation more highly than do middle school teachers with general types of preparation (Scales and McEwin, 1994) and that the specifically trained middle school teachers have more positive attitudes toward teaching at this level (Stahler, 1995). A positive attitude toward teaching students may indeed be important, given that middle school teachers have lower retention rates (83 percent stayed at the same school from the 1993–1994 school year to the next) than either elementary (86 percent retained) or high school (88 percent retained) school teachers (Alt and Choy, 2000).[4]

There have also been recent efforts to link middle school training programs to improved student achievement. Mertens, Flowers, and Mulhall have investigated the link between interdisciplinary team teaching and student achievement, on one hand, and the link between classroom practices and student achievement, on the other hand. They have demonstrated that middle school certification is associated with greater use of teaming practices (Mertens, Flowers, and Mulhall, 2002). In their earlier work, Mertens, Flowers, and Mulhall (1998) reported that higher percentage of students at schools that had implemented interdisciplinary teaming reached the "sat-

---

[4]However, in SASS 2001 (NCES, 1999–2000 school year, 37 percent of the middle school teachers responded that they certainly would become a teacher again; only 5 percent responded that they certainly would not become a teacher again. There was no statistically significant difference between the responses of those teaching at middle schools and those teaching at elementary or high schools, indicating similar levels of satisfaction among these groups. However, it is unknown whether these respondents are satisfied with their current grade-level assignment.

isfactory" performance level on the statewide achievement test than did at schools with lower levels of implementation.

Despite these early indications that middle school certification may benefit teachers and students, it is not clear whether training specific to middle school should be *required* of all prospective teachers at these grade levels. Although teachers at this grade level should be able to implement instructional practices that are appropriate for the students' developmental stage, it is not clear whether middle school–specific training is the only way to reach this goal.

Professional development provides the opportunity to train teachers on both subject matter and adolescent-specific pedagogical methodologies that many middle school teachers have missed in their preparation programs. In the next section of this chapter, we describe the professional development currently offered to middle school teachers and discuss the issues related to this training.

Professional Development for Middle School Teachers

As with teacher preparation, experts tend to agree that teachers should engage in professional development in their subject matter and in subject-matter pedagogy, ensuring that teachers can integrate standards and use assessments to improve student performance (Desimone et al., 2002). Middle school advocates agree that professional development should focus on curriculum and instruction but add that programs should also cover adolescent development, classroom management, service learning, interdisciplinary teaming, and parent involvement (Jackson and Davis, 2000; Mizell, 2002; Flowers, Mertens, and Mulhall, 2002).[5] Adolescent development—and, to some extent, interdisciplinary teaming—may be the only items on the list that are unique to middle schools.

In examining professional development at the K–12 level in 30 schools in 10 districts in five states, Desimone et al. (2002) found that most professional development not only did not focus on content but was traditionally structured, lasted less than a week, was not aligned with standards, and was offered to individuals rather than to entire departments or teacher groups. Middle school reformers and advocates concur that most professional development at the middle school level is disparate, fragmented, and unconnected to teachers' classroom experiences and needs (Mizell, 2002; Jackson and Davis, 2000).

---

[5]Killion (1999) provides a list of content-based professional development programs that have been demonstrated to improve student achievement.

Latest Models of Professional Development

Experts also are coming to agree on the important structural approaches to providing professional development. Accordingly, it has been argued that in-service training should be in-depth, active, aligned to curriculum standards, of extended duration, and embedded in teachers' daily work—ideally, groups of teachers from the same district, school, or department should participate collectively (Desimone et al., 2002; Lipsitz, Jackson, et al., 1997; Jackson and Davis, 2000; Mizell, 2002). Researchers are urging schools to move away from traditional workshop-orientated professional development toward more-integrated school-based forms of professional development. Professional development appears to be particularly beneficial when it is conducted in the schools with groups of teachers and administrators together, with an emphasis on context-specific strategies; with multiple opportunities for teachers to practice what they are learning; and with structured, built-in time for reflection and experimentation (Elmore, 2002; King, 2002; Knight, 2002; Lieberman, 1995; Lieberman and Wood, 2001).

SASS Analyses on Professional Development

One recent SASS analysis offers a glimpse of professional development activities at all grade levels. The respondent pool included 38,375 teachers. Of these, 4,527 were teaching at schools with grades at or between the 5th- and 8th-grade levels only.[6] Our analyses focused on the professional development that middle school teachers engaged in and the differences in professional development experiences among elementary, middle, and high school teachers.[7]

Our results confirm that professional development is ubiquitous at the middle school level, with 93 percent of the middle school respondents having attended a workshop in the past 12 months and 32 percent having taken a university course in the past 12 months for certification purposes. However, these two activities are quite traditional; these data do not indicate whether teachers at the middle school level are engaging in the integrated, school-based training that experts advocate.

The SASS data provided us some insights on the content of professional development in which middle school teachers are participating. Table 7.2 lists the percentages of middle school teachers engaging in specific types of professional development, along with the number of hours they did so in the past 12 months and the percentages who found such training useful. As shown in the table, approximately 70 percent of middle school teachers reported having received training in the instruc-

---

[6]We defined middle schools as those including grades 5–8, 6–8, and 7–8; elementary as including grades K–5 and K–6; and high school as including grades 9–12 and 10–12.

[7]We used weighted data in running frequencies, correlations, and regressions. Statistically significant differences were considered at the 0.01 level.

Table 7.2
Teacher Participation in Professional Development

Content	% of Those Surveyed Who Had Participated	Time Spent (hours)	Found Participation Very Useful (%)	Would Like to Do More (%)[a]
Uses of computers for instruction	71	9–16	32	60
Teaching methods	71	9–16	24	36
Content and performance standards in main teaching field	69	9–16	20	43
Student assessment	62	9–16	18	33
In-depth study of content in main teaching field	54	9–16	30	47
Student discipline and classroom management	42	0–8	20	9

SOURCE: SASS (2001) data on teacher participation in professional development activities over the preceding 12 months.
[a]The survey asked teachers to list their top three priorities for additional professional development. The percentages here represent teachers who chose the given content area among their top three choices. These areas may therefore not be the only ones in which teachers desire professional development.

tional use of computers, teaching methods, and content and performance standards. In fact, they were more likely to receive training in computer use, teaching methods, standards, and student assessment than in their main teaching subject. Unfortunately, these data do not show whether teachers received training on how to teach their content—something researchers specifically recommend (Killion, 1999). Also, less than half had received training in classroom management. In light of our earlier review on student behavior problems (in Chapter Four), classroom management appears to be an important topic for professional development.

While the number of hours of professional development were all quite modest (most typically 9 to 12 hours per year), the low ratings of the usefulness were even more striking. *Only 18 to 32 percent of middle school teachers reported finding the various topics of professional development very useful.* With the exception of computer use, most middle school teachers were not eager to receive additional training on these topics. About one-third of teachers listed teaching methods and student assessment as their top three choices for additional professional development, and less than one-tenth of the teachers chose training on student behavioral problems among their top three areas for future professional development. It should be noted, however, that close to one-half the teachers expressed interest in additional training in the content of their main teaching field.

When we examined differences in professional development across various school characteristics (by size, location, student poverty level, percentage of ethnic minority students, etc.), we found few differences. However, teachers in rural middle schools were less likely to engage in three areas of professional development: study of content in main teaching field, content and performance standards, and pedagogy. Further research may be warranted to determine whether schools in remote locations have adequate access to professional development.

We also compared professional development across middle, elementary, and high schools. As Table 7.3 shows, elementary school teachers are more likely to engage in professional development in all areas listed, with the exception of educational technology, than are either middle or high school teachers. Compared to high school teachers, middle school teachers were more likely to have undergone professional development on standards, assessment, and subject matter.

There were also statistically significant differences between elementary and middle school teachers in the amount of support provided to new teachers, who typically need the support the most. SASS asked teachers whether they received a range of support during their first year of teaching. We found that elementary schools teachers were more likely to have received such support as common planning time, mentoring, and extra classroom assistance during their first year than were middle school teachers (Table 7.4).[8] No type of first-year support was more likely to have been provided to middle school teachers than to elementary school teachers.

In sum, current evidence suggests that existing professional development at the middle school level is fragmented and traditional. Furthermore, it seems that elementary school teachers receive more support, both during their first year in the profession and in continuing professional development, than do middle school teachers.

Challenges, Recommendations, and Exploratory Ideas

As the interest in teacher quality increases, it is important to consider how teachers are prepared before they enter the teaching field and how they are trained throughout their careers. Middle schools face two major challenges related to teacher training. *One major challenge is how to ensure that middle school teachers are well trained in their subject areas.* One goal of the NCLB legislation is to improve the quality of middle school teaching. Given that the percentage of teachers teaching in their subject at the middle school level has not changed substantially since 1988, either there are not enough of these teachers in the labor pool, or middle schools have lacked incentives to hire them or assign them to their areas of expertise. In the future, more middle schools might recruit from the pool of teachers trained for the high school level or from alternative pools of people with mathematics and science backgrounds. *States, districts, and schools should benefit from an analysis of their hiring practices to ensure that*

---

[8]High school teachers were even less likely than middle school teachers to receive common planning time during their first year of teaching, but there were no other differences between high school and elementary teachers on these support variables.

Table 7.3

Percentages of Elementary, Middle, and High School Teachers Engaging in Professional Development in Past Year

	Elementary (%)	Middle (%)	High (%)
Teaching methods	79	71	NA
Content and performance standards in main teaching field	82	69	65
Student assessment	71	62	55
In-depth study of content in main teaching field	68	54	50

Table 7.4

Percentages of Elementary and Middle School Teachers Receiving Support in Their First Year of Teaching

	Elementary (%)	Middle (%)
Provided with common planning time	54	40
Worked with a mentor	66	60
Received extra classroom assistance	31	24

there are sufficient incentives to attract subject-matter specialists to teaching posts at the middle school level.

If recruiting from nontraditional pools increases, it is even less likely that new middle school teachers will have had formal education on the developmental characteristics of young teens or that whatever such education the teachers have had will relate to everyday classroom practices. *The second major challenge middle schools face therefore centers on how these teachers can obtain training that helps them effectively manage and instruct young teens.* In light of our findings in previous chapters, middle school teachers might benefit most from learning about effective classroom management techniques for this age group. In addition, partnerships with local teacher-training institutions would allow student teachers to conduct their fieldwork in a middle school, providing a natural laboratory—that should be coupled with theoretical coursework—for learning about students at this developmental stage.

Given that many teachers at this grade level currently lack subject-and/or adolescent-specific knowledge, ongoing professional development for middle school teachers may be the most feasible mechanism for improving teaching quality in middle schools. Additional training in subject-matter knowledge, content-specific pedagogy,[9] and adolescent developmental issues could be delivered to middle school teachers in formats that reflect current evidence-based recommendations. Training providers for the middle school level need to be especially sensitive to the issue of differing teacher capacities, given that these teachers represent a mix of training backgrounds. *States, districts, and*

---

[9]Trimble (2003) provides examples of evidence-based teaching strategies.

schools should ensure that there are sufficient resources to provide this training, as well as strong incentives to encourage teachers to engage in the professional development they need.

By researching the effects of professional development programs on student outcomes (achievement, motivation, disciplinary problems), researchers can suggest improvements to teacher education. While it makes intuitive sense that teachers should understand the developmental needs of their students, there is little research to explain exactly what this means. What should teachers be taught about young adolescents? Is there generalizable information about students at this age that would help teachers improve how they plan or deliver lessons? How does such training relate to academic achievement, level of engagement, or classroom climate? For example, evaluations of professional development programs and preservice training that educate teachers about their students' developmental needs could provide valuable information to guide future training. Researchers would not only have to delineate the links between specific training components and instructional techniques but also between instructional techniques and student achievement. If gains in student achievement are demonstrated, middle school advocates would be better prepared to argue for changes in the current teacher education system. In addition, researchers should continue to test and compare various models of teacher preparation (for example middle school–specific versus high school–specific with subsequent professional development on adolescent development) for their effects on student achievement. Appendix D provides some examples of such research.

CHAPTER EIGHT

Parental Involvement

Most educators and parents believe that a child's academic success and adaptive functioning in school are related not only to how well principals run the schools and how capably teachers teach but also to the degree to which parents get involved in their children's schooling. However, the association between parental involvement and student performance is complex and varies depending on the type of involvement being considered. The goal of this chapter is to shed light on the connection between parental involvement and student achievement. We are particularly interested in the concern that parental involvement drops off when students transition into middle school and the effects the decline in involvement might have on students' academic success. Among the questions this chapter addresses are the following

- What does *parental involvement* mean?
- Does parental involvement matter? Does it contribute to students' academic achievement?
- What factors might account for the decline in parental involvement in the middle school years?
- What are schools doing to encourage parents to stay involved?

The Many Forms of Parental Involvement

Parental involvement is complex and encompasses a broad range of parental behaviors, such as monitoring the child, communicating with schools, and helping with homework. Epstein (1995) developed what is now a well-known categorization of parent involvement that reflects its many dimensions:

1. Are parents meeting their basic obligation to provide for the safety and health of their children?
2. Is the school meeting its basic obligation to communicate with families about school programs and the individual progress of their children?
3. Do parents involve themselves in school activities?
4. Do parents assist in learning activities at home?

5. Do parents involve themselves in decisionmaking at school?
6. Do parents have opportunities for collaboration and exchanges with community organizations to increase family and student access to community resources and service?

Other authors, such as Ho and Willms (1996), have categorized parental involvement by the specific behaviors parents perform, such as discussions with children at home, supervision of children at home, communication with the school, and participation at the school.

Although it is usually presumed that parents directly affect their children's school success, parental influence also may be indirect. Falbo, Lein, and Amador (2001) point to the importance of the indirect linkage. They contend that parents play a major role in their children's education because—intentionally or not—they choose the school the child will attend. While some parents are in a position to select a neighborhood specifically to get their children into its schools, others have less or no choice. Regardless of the degree to which the parents can choose among different schools or the degree to which they have made a deliberate choice to send their child to a particular school, they are determining the teachers and peers to whom their children will be exposed.

When parents of middle school students are involved, what are they most likely to do? To study this question, Epstein and Lee (1995) analyzed NELS:88 data on 8th graders. Table 8.1 provides specific results of their findings for three data sources: parents, students, and principals. As shown in the table,

- Almost all parents reported having rules about homework, but only about one-half the students said that their parents often check their homework.
- About one-half the parents reported that they had never contacted the school about their child's performance, but less than one-third of the students were under the impression that their parents had talked to a teacher or counselor during the school year.
- The majority of the students reported that their parents had not visited their class during the school year, and the majority of the principals reported that only 10 percent or fewer parents volunteer at their school.
- Only one-quarter of the principals reported that most of their parents receive information about how to help their children at home.

The researchers noted that their findings accord well with other research on this topic (Epstein and Lee, 1995, p. 147):

> about 20 percent of families remain active and knowledgeable partners with their children's schools. Most middle grade schools in the nation give little information to families, and most families give little assistance about school to their children in the middle grades.

Table 8.1
Parent, Principal, and Student Perceptions of Parental Involvement Based on NELS:88 Data

Respondents	Report About Parental Involvement	Frequency (%)
Parents	Never contacted about their child's academic program	65
	Never contacted about their child's academic performance	45
	Never contacted about their child's behavior	69
	Have rules about homework	92
	Place limits on TV viewing	84
	Never contacted their school about child's behavior	71
Principals	Report fewer than 10% of families attend workshops on school programs, adolescent development or other child-rearing topics	83
	Report that 10% or fewer parents volunteer at their schools	71
	Report that most of their parents receive information on how to help at home	25
Students	Parents did not talk to a teacher or counselor by phone or in person during the school year	30
	Parents often check whether they have done their homework	45
	Families attended some events in which they participated at school	63
	Parents did not visit their class during the school year	70
	Discussed class work with their parents more than twice during the year	66

SOURCE: Epstein and Lee (1995).

Parent Involvement and Student Achievement

Although there is a substantial body of research on parental involvement, only a smaller subset focuses on young teens or the middle school years. Yet, developmental psychologists (e.g, Steinberg, 1990) contend that it is particularly important for parents to be involved with the lives of their children during this phase and, in particular, during the transition to middle school (Lord, Eccles, and McCarthy, 1994). Research on parent-teen relationships shows that close connections and communication between parents and young teens are associated with better school performance and psychosocial adjustment (Steinberg, Elmen, and Mounts, 1989). One way to facilitate this closeness is for parents to be knowledgeable about and involved in their children's school activities and schoolwork. Several studies show that, when parents do not monitor and stay involved, their young teens are at elevated risk for compromised school achievement and conduct problems (Jessor and Jessor, 1977).

We provide an overview of some recent reviews examining the question of whether parental involvement is associated with academic success. While not all of these pertain to middle schools in particular, they do help us illustrate the lack of consensus in this field of research more accurately.

A number of the reviews sum up the research on the effects of parental involvement on student achievement as being overwhelmingly positive (Henderson and Mapp, 2002), while others are more hesitant to make causal conclusions

(Thorkildsen and Scott Stein, 1998). For example, Henderson and Mapp (2002, p. 24) reviewed 51 studies and concluded that

> Taken as a whole, these studies found a positive and convincing relationship between family involvement and benefits for students, including academic achievement. This relationship holds across families of all economic, racial/ethnic, and educational backgrounds and for students at all ages.

However, the statistically significant positive effects are generally small, and in some cases, the association is negative, with lower scores or grades related to higher levels of involvement. The authors typically explain these negative associations by noting that parents get involved when their children have academic or behavioral problems.

The NMSA Research Summary on Parent Involvement and Student Achievement at the Middle Level (NMSA, 2000) points out inconsistencies in research results, with some studies not finding statistically significant links between parent involvement and achievement. The summary also concludes that findings have been mixed across different racial and economic groups.

Like the NMSA, Thorkildsen and Scott Stein (1998) are critical of the parent involvement literature. They assert that "many researchers overinterpret their findings of statistical significance" and that "causal relationships are implied from correlational studies." They based their conclusions on reviews of over 50 articles, reviews, and studies, many of which were published in peer-reviewed publications. We agree with the limited evidence regarding causality. Few studies even discuss the possibility that the positive association between parental involvement and academic performance could be due to parents of academically excelling students being more likely to get and stay involved in school.

To provide some examples of studies, we will next review three investigations that used NELS:88 data to examine the association between parental involvement and student achievement in the 8th grade by relying on different informants. Keith and Keith (1993) analyzed parent and student responses in the NELS:88 data and concluded that parental involvement is associated with 8th-grade learning across different subject areas. They found positive associations between the amount of parental involvement and student success. Also, direct involvement with children, such as encouraging homework and academic pursuits, was more likely than parental involvement in the school to influence student achievement.

Ho and Willms (1996) also used NELS:88 data from 8th graders to compare how parental behavior at home and parental actions at school influenced achievement. They found that home discussion of school activities was positively related to the students' achievement in reading and mathematics. No such correlation was found for school participation (such as attending parent-teacher organization meetings or volunteering in the classroom). The authors concluded that participation at the home may be the most beneficial to the child directly.

However, parental involvement at school might have different long-term implications for student achievement. Trusty (1999) examined how students' plans for their post–high school careers related to parental involvement. He found that students' expectations to pursue a bachelor's degree were positively associated with parents' involvement at home and in parent-teacher organizations. This suggests that parental involvement shows the student that education is a valuable and worthwhile goal. This interpretation remains as a hypothesis, however, because other variables, such as students' grades, could also affect the student's expectations. For example, if the parents of one child were highly involved at school and at home, that child might have higher grades than if the parents were not involved. With higher grades, that student might see a bachelor's degree as more achievable than would a student whose parents were not involved and who did not receive good grades. Thus, although it is difficult to pinpoint exactly what it is about the parents' involvement that would link to student achievement expectations, the study nevertheless reinforces the findings of other studies demonstrating a connection between parental involvement and academic performance.

Declining Parental Involvement

Do parents stay involved in their children's education after the children leave elementary school? Knowing whether parental involvement actually declines between elementary school and middle school would illuminate how parental involvement might contribute to the decline in student achievement between the elementary and middle school years.

Eccles and Harold (1996) examined the effects of grade level and school structure on parental involvement. They sampled students in the 2nd, 3rd, and 5th grades to see how involvement differed in those grade levels. They were also able to examine the effects of school structure because some of the 5th graders were in elementary school, while others were in middle schools. In general, they found that rates of parental involvement, as defined by the amount of volunteering in school, declined from 2nd to 5th grade. However, there was a significant drop between elementary and middle school, so that the decline in the 5th grade was greater for those in middle schools. Thus, school structure itself appears to make a difference in the degree to which parents are involved with their children's schooling.

In analysis of two surveys that explored practices in both elementary and middle schools (the NCES Survey on Family and School Partnerships in Public Schools,

K–8[1] and the National Household Education Surveys Program's Parent and Family Involvement in Education/Civic Involvement Survey[2]), Chen (2001) found that different forms of parental involvement (besides volunteering in school) declined between elementary and middle school (see Figures 8.1, 8.2, and 8.3). As the graphs show, parents of middle school students appear to receive less information about helping with their schoolwork and attend fewer teacher-parent conferences and school-sponsored activities less often than do parents of elementary school students.

Figure 8.1
Percentage of Public Schools That Reported Providing Information and Percentage of Parents That Reported Receiving Information on How to Help with Homework, by School Level in 1996

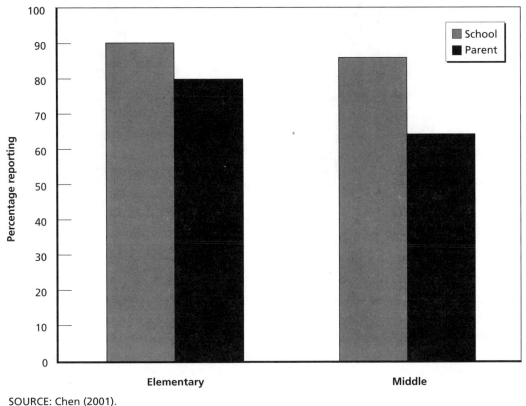

SOURCE: Chen (2001).
RAND *MG139-8.1*

---

[1]This survey defined an elementary school as one beginning with 4th grade or lower and having no grade higher than 8 and middle school as one that begins with 5th grade or higher and has no grade higher than 8.

[2]This survey defined an elementary school as one whose lowest grade was K, 1, 2, 3, or 4 and a middle school as one whose lowest grade was 5, 6, 7, or 8.

Figure 8.2
Percentage of Public Schools Reporting Most or All Parents Having Attended and Percentage of Parents Reporting Having Attended Parent-Teacher Conferences, by School Level in 1996

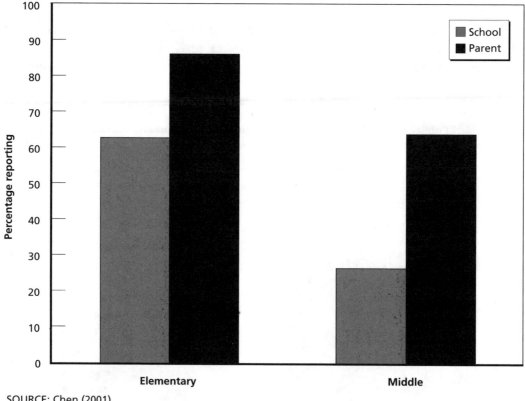

SOURCE: Chen (2001).
RAND *MG139-8.2*

Interestingly, schools reported that they supply parents with more information and opportunities than parents reported receiving, and parents reported that they are more involved than schools reported them to be.

Several factors could affect this apparent decline between elementary and middle school. One is the difference in school organizations: Teachers in elementary school have 20 to 30 students, but middle school teachers often have over 100 students (Dornbush and Glasgow, 1996). The large number of students is likely to affect the teacher's ability (and motivation) to reach out to the parents for their continued involvement. Similarly, parents might not know which teacher to approach if they wanted to be in contact with the school. Dauber and Epstein (1989) point out that changes in parents' perceptions of their children and of their own ability to assist their children are a major influence on the extent to which the parents will stay involved. First, parents' belief in their own efficacy, such as in their ability to help

Figure 8.3
Percentage of Public Schools Reporting Most or All Parents Attending Open House or Back-to-School Nights, and Percentage of Parents Reporting Having Attended Such Events, by School Level in 1996

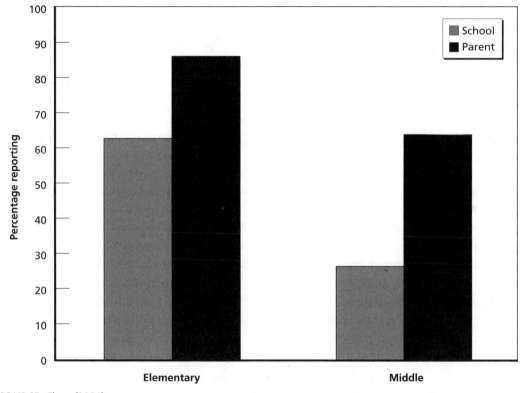

SOURCE: Chen (2001).
RAND *MG139-8.3*

their children with homework, may decline. For example, as the homework becomes increasingly difficult, parents might become discouraged and withdraw their involvement. In addition, parents who believe that children need more independence once they enter the middle grades may assume that their involvement should decline to accommodate their children's changing needs.

Another factor that is likely to contribute to parents' lack of involvement in middle school is parents' general knowledge of their children's schooling. Mulhall, Mertens, and Flowers (2001) found that parents are not very knowledgeable about middle school practices. As Table 8.2 shows, few parents consider themselves to be very familiar with a number of the practices that are considered key pieces of middle school reform and practiced at least to some degree in the schools in the study sample. If parents do not understand the school's structure or practices, they may feel ill-equipped to get involved in the process.

Table 8.2
Parents' Familiarity with Middle-Grade Practices

	Not at All Familiar	A Little Familiar	Somewhat Familiar	Very Familiar
Interdisciplinary teaming	42	17	20	20
Advisory programs	52	18	17	13
Integrated lessons	43	22	21	14
Heterogeneous grouping	41	20	21	18
Exploratory activities	29	25	27	20
Cooperative learning	24	24	28	24

SOURCE: Mulhall, Mertens, and Flowers (2001), p. 58.

SASS Analysis of Parental Involvement in Elementary, Middle, and High Schools

To further examine the assumption of declining parental involvement, we analyzed data from the most recent 2001 SASS. In the SASS school survey, principals were asked about parent involvement in two separate sets of questions. First, when asked specifically about their means of facilitating parent participation at the school (for example, open houses or back-to-school nights, parent-teacher conferences, parent education workshops or courses), respondents, on average, marked 6.8 (75 percent) of the nine options listed. Second, a similar follow-up question asked whether the school had such things as a staff member assigned to work on parent involvement; a log of parent participation; or requirements that teachers send information home, provide activities for parents, or create homework that involves parents. Respondents only marked an average of 2.7 (33 percent) of the eight options. Examples from the two sets of questions are listed below in Table 8.3.

As with our other analyses on the SASS data (see Chapters Five and Six), we analyzed differences between elementary, middle, and high schools. As Table 8.3 indicates, almost all middle schools reported providing general events for parents, such as back-to-school nights and specific subject-area events. However, these data also show that middle schools offered 20 percent fewer workshops and courses than did elementary schools. Interestingly, parents volunteered only 10 percent less in middle school than in elementary school, but the drop was 17 percent between middle and high schools. These data suggest that parental in-school involvement might not decline as much between elementary and middle school as earlier studies suggested, although these data do not indicate that fewer parents were involved.

Schools' efforts to facilitate parental involvement typically declined by 10 to 15 percent between elementary and middle schools. However, Table 8.3 shows, 27 percent fewer middle schools than elementary schools report offering services to support parental involvement, such as providing child care. Although such services are even less prevalent at the high school level (only 17 percent of high schools offer them), the difference might have different implications for parents: Parents with younger children are able to attend school events when they can leave them with siblings who are high school age, but cannot necessarily leave younger children with middle school age siblings. It should also be noted that only 37 percent of the middle schools (compared with almost 50 percent of the elementary schools) reported requiring teachers to provide suggestions for activities that parents could do at home with their children. Thus, the level of specific assistance and support for parental involvement in school and at home does indeed decline between elementary and middle school.

In sum, there appear to be reliable differences in the degrees to which schools facilitate parental involvement and the degrees to which parents are involved across elementary and middle schools. It is difficult to determine from the available data whether or not parents are less involved because they are less interested, but schools also seem to contribute to the decline by offering fewer activities and providing less help.

When we analyzed differences across different middle schools by examining the effects of whom they serve, we found that the size of school enrollment and the percentage of ethnic minority students correlated positively with the number of types of events and services provided. Thus, the SASS data suggest that larger middle schools and those with larger numbers of ethnic minority students offer more programs to facilitate parent involvement. This finding may reflect the ways schools reach out to parents or may reflect a greater need to reach out.

Table 8.3
Prevalence of Different Types of Parent Involvement by School Level

Does the School Have the Following?	Elementary	Middle	High
Open house or back-to-school night	98.2	97.7	88.2
Regularly scheduled schoolwide parent-teacher conferences	95.8	84.1	72.3
Special subject-area events (such as science fair and concerts)	90.1	94.0	78.4
Parent education workshops or courses	64.0	48.4	37.1
Written contract between school and parent	52.2	50.7	46.7
Parents as volunteers at the school	97.3	87.9	70.5
Parents involved in instructional issues	74.5	65.1	62.7
Parents involved in governance	64.2	62.4	55.2
Parents involved in budget decisions	51.6	43.1	37.8
Staff member assigned to work on parent involvement	61.3	50.7	43.9
A log of parent participation maintained by parents or staff	77.8	63.1	46.3
A reliable system of communication with parents (such as newsletters)	98.3	95.9	91.0
Services to support parent participation (such as child care)	49.4	22.7	16.9
A parent drop-in center or lounge	26.8	17.4	11.0
Requirement that teachers send info home to parents explaining lessons	60.5	56.1	47.0
A requirement that teachers provide suggestions for activities that parents can do at home with their child	54.2	37.5	22.3

SOURCE: 2001 SASS.

These findings suggest that middle schools could improve parental involvement by offering more workshops and courses, suggesting activities that parents can do at home with their children, and providing support services that would allow parents to come to school.

Factors That Influence Parental Involvement

Many factors affect parents' ability to help with and their interest in their children's schooling. Some factors that can confound the effects of parental involvement include the characteristics and life circumstances of the parents. For example, parents who have inflexible work hours have trouble being involved in school. In an Eccles and Harold (1996) study, the most frequent reason parents of 7th graders cited for lack of involvement was work commitments (62 percent). Although many cannot come to school, this does not mean that they do not want to be involved. In the same study, Eccles and Harold found that 86 percent of the parents of 7th graders agreed that schools are more effective when parents are involved.

A number of researchers have used NELS:88 data to explore how parental involvement varies across different demographic groups and how it varies for parents of boys and girls. For example, Ho and Willms (1996) found few differences in parental involvement in schools or at home across SES and ethnic groups. Using the same NELS:88 data, Keith and Keith (1993) found that higher-SES parents were more involved than others and that parents of African-American, Hispanic, and Native American origin reported more involvement than those from other ethnic groups. Thus, there appear to be some SES and ethnic differences in parental involvement, but they are not consistent across studies—even those that rely on the same data.

There is also evidence to suggest that involvement varies between parents of boys and girls. Ho and Willms (1996) found some gender differences. Parents tended to talk more often directly with a daughter, but tended to talk more often with a son's teachers. Carter and Wojtkiewicz (2000) also found gender differences in the NELS:88 data. Their analyses showed that parents were more involved with daughters in some ways and more with sons in other ways. For example, parents are more likely to check their son's homework than their daughter's.

Schools should attend to variations among parents of different socioeconomic status and between parents of boys and girls. School staff may need to target specific groups of parents using different means. But what do schools need to do to get parents involved?

Schools' Efforts to Get Parents Involved

Given the extensive interest in encouraging parental involvement and the complexity of the process, many schools, districts, states, and the federal government (through provisions in NCLB) have funded and/or required programs or services that facilitate parental involvement. Additionally, numerous university-based research centers (for example, the Center on School, Family, and Community Partnerships at Johns Hopkins University) and nonprofit organizations and information clearinghouses (for example, the National Parent Information Network, the National Coalition for Parent Involvement, the National Parent Teacher Association (PTA)) are devoted to increasing parental involvement and making people more aware of its potential benefits. While we have named some programs here, this is not a comprehensive list, but rather a sample of organizations working in this arena.

Because the concept of including parents is so popular, we offer the following example.[3] According to Williams and Chavkin (1989), good parent-involvement programs feature the following elements:

- written policies, because they demonstrate that parent involvement is considered a priority and spell out features and goals
- administrative support for the programs, including funding, such resources as space and materials, and staff time
- training for teachers on how to structure and utilize parental involvement
- partnerships and communication between parents and the school, so that they can both work together and stay informed about planning, goals, and developing issues
- networking with other schools to compare parent-involvement issues
- periodic evaluations, to ensure that goals are being met.

The National PTA has also developed standards for teacher credential programs to use in training teachers how to better facilitate parent involvement((quoted from National PTA, 1998):

- **Standard I:** Communicating—Communication between home and school is regular, two-way, and meaningful.
- **Standard II:** Parenting—Parenting skills are promoted and supported.
- **Standard III:** Student Learning—Parents play an integral role in assisting student learning.
- **Standard IV:** Volunteering— Parents are welcome in the school, and their support and assistance are sought.
- **Standard V:** School Decision Making and Advocacy—Parents are full partners in the decisions that affect children and families.

---

[3] See the References for Web addresses for these organizations.

- **Standard VI:** Collaborating with Community—Community resources are used to strengthen schools, families, and student learning.

In addition, there are examples of specific programs that schools can use to facilitate parental involvement. Researchers at Johns Hopkins University, in conjunction with teachers from a number of nearby states, extended the Teachers Involve Parents in Schoolwork (TIPS) program from elementary to middle grades. They have created interactive homework problems in language arts, science, and mathematics, which require students to solicit input from someone at home to complete the homework assignment successfully. A summary of the TIPS evaluation (Epstein, Simon, and Salinas, 1997) indicates that:

> parent participation in TIPS added significantly to students' writing scores as the year progressed; doing more TIPS homework positively affected language arts report card grades at the end of the school year; students with lower report card grades were more positive about TIPS than were more successful students, indicating that TIPS may help keep some of these students engaged in homework even if they do not like school very much, parents who monitored their children's grades and who participated more often with their children liked the TIPS process more than did other parents.

Challenges, Recommendations, and Exploratory Ideas

Parental involvement in education is of great interest to the scientific and educational communities, as well as to parents themselves. As noted, an example of the trend toward increased awareness of this topic is NCLB's inclusion of provisions relating to parental involvement. NCLB mandates that schools inform parents about teacher qualifications and about supplementary programs for students. However, these steps provide minimal information about the schools and therefore are not sufficient to get parents involved or to benefit the child *directly*.

Parental involvement can take many forms, and some home-based activities, such as help with homework and discussions about school events, are especially likely to be associated with higher student achievement. This association can, however, lead to different conclusions: That parental input helps students (the typical conclusion) or that parents of students who do well in school are more likely to be involved in their children's education. The latter option is rarely discussed. Appendix D proposes ways in which this question could be tested to gain a better understanding of the "causal" nature of this relation. In the absence of such research, we recommend that middle schools engage parents more actively because of the findings that a *lack of* parental involvement is likely to be associated with low academic achievement and behavior problems. Hence, *we conclude that, although parental involvement is not nec-*

essarily sufficient to bring about academic success, its absence may increase the risk of school difficulties.

Also, even if parental involvement does not cause students to excel academically, increased participation of parents in the school lives of children might be beneficial in other ways. Developmental research suggests that supportive relationships between parents and young teens *are particularly important socially and emotionally when young teens are going through developmental changes and as they transition to a new school (see Chapters Two and Five).* It seems to be common sense that parents need to understand the goals and practices of the school (for example, by knowing the meaning of terms used to refer to school practices, such as teaming, advisories, and homeroom periods) to be able to discuss school issues with their young teens or to be in contact with the school. Therefore, *we suggest that, at minimum, middle schools make sure that all parents receive factual information about the school's goals and practices.* We recognize that such information is not likely to be sufficient to bring about changes in parental behavior or student outcomes, but it may provide the necessary foundation for communication.

Our analyses of the national SASS data suggest that, *although middle school principals perceive the lack of parental involvement to be a problem (see Chapter Six), middle schools do little to actively encourage it.* We found that fewer than one-half of middle schools offer any workshops and courses for parents, and only little more than one-third of public middle schools require teachers to provide suggestions for activities that parents can do at home with their children. Yet, the middle school years are likely to be when parents would most welcome workshops on developmental changes and the implications of such changes for parent-child relationships, emerging risky behaviors, and academic performance. Specifically, the middle school years may be when parents most need advice on how best to help or how to be supportive in a manner that does not infringe on young teens' desire to be independent. *We recommend that middle schools experiment with different types of activities and supports to foster better communication between home and school.* Although such efforts should be evaluated, it might be unreasonable to expect all forms of parental involvement to increase academic outcomes. Hence, additional indicators, such as changes in discipline problems, also need to be included in such evaluations.

Although our analyses of the international comparison of the HBSC data (Chapter Five) shows that middle school students consider their parents to be relatively involved and supportive, this does not necessarily mean that their parents are *partners* with their schools and teachers. *Partnerships, defined as shared knowledge and expectations between parents and teachers, should be the ultimate goal for enhancing the school success and well-being of our young teens.*

CHAPTER NINE

Whole-School Reform Models

Many innovations and programs have been designed to improve student outcomes and address other perceived problems at the middle school level, but most have been implemented in too piecemeal a fashion (Beane, 2001) to lead to widespread and lasting change. So, the following are among the questions this chapter will address:

- What are some of the major reform efforts at work in middle schools?
- What are their goals and primary features?
- Do the reforms show promise for addressing the challenges middle schools face today?

The Comprehensive School Reform Program (CSR) provides federal funds to help schools implement and sustain comprehensive reforms, also known as whole-school reform efforts. Comprehensive models or designs are characterized by alignment of all of the educational system's components (its curriculum, instruction, assessment, professional development, financial resources, governance, and community involvement) toward a common goal of improving student learning (North Central Regional Educational Laboratory [NCREL], 1998). CSR targets high-poverty and low-performing schools, especially those receiving Title I funds.

CSR has identified 11 components of reform that comprehensive models should include. The components are organized around three overarching themes: Models must be grounded in scientifically based research, must provide evidence of effectiveness in improving student achievement, and must be replicable on a larger scale (NCREL, 1998). CSR has affected middle school reform efforts by providing federal funding to help several models scale up their programs.

This chapter focuses on six CSR programs that have been implemented in middle schools:

- Different Ways of Knowing (DWOK)
- Turning Points Transforming Middle Schools (Turning Points)
- Making Middle Grades Work[1]

---

[1] Formerly called Making Middle Grades Matter.

- Middle Start
- The Talent Development Middle School Model (TDMS)
- AIM at Middle Grades Results (AIM).

Below, we will describe each reform model and briefly review what is known about its effectiveness.

Although other whole-school reform models are being implemented in middle schools (e.g., Success for All and Comer's School Development Program), we have focused on the particular models highlighted by the National Forum to Accelerate Middle Grades Reform.

The models have similar goals, but they differ with respect to specific features or emphasis on particular activities. In our analysis we examined several dimensions of the six reforms:

- **Goals:** What goals are the reforms trying to achieve?
- **Focus:** What part of the school experience (e.g., academics, assessment, pedagogy) does the reform effort target?
- **Reform activities:** Does the reform involve some of the core practices of the middle school concept reviewed in Chapter Three (e.g., flexible scheduling, interdisciplinary team teaching, advisory programs)?
- **Content:** What is the academic content of the reform effort?
- **Support from reform group:** Does the sponsoring group offer written documentation, technical assistance, professional development, etc., to help the school with implementation?
- **Organizational supports:** Does implementing the reform require organizational changes?
- **Evaluation:** Has the reform been evaluated, and if so, what were the findings?

We relied on publicly available documentation to describe each reform. Specifically, our descriptions are based on (1) information gathered from each reform's Web site, (2) descriptions of the reforms at the Web sites of the National Forum to Accelerate Middle School Reform, Northwest Regional Educational Laboratory's Catalog of School Reform Model Web site, and Edsource On-Line School Reform Model's Overview, (3) a library search of evaluations conducted of these reforms, and in some cases, (4) materials obtained from the sponsoring organization. Our intent is to provide an overview of the reforms, highlighting features of the models that are designed to promote their goals.[2] We encourage readers who are interested in more details of a particular model to visit its Web site or contact its program developer.

---

[2]The Web sources we list provide varying degrees of details for each reform model. All models, for example, promote a healthy school climate, but some Web sites provide specific examples of how this is done and others do not. For this reason, if a particular feature (for example, advisory programs) is not included as part of a model's description, we cannot presume that the model necessarily excludes this feature.

The following tables summarize the key information for each reform model, including its prevalence, major goals, key elements, and provisions for services and support. An examination of these tables suggests there is much consensus in the goals of the middle school reform models profiled. Although they have different means of reaching their objectives, each model aims *to improve student achievement, promote social equity, and enhance developmental responsiveness.* All the reform models also provide coaching, consultation, and technical assistance, as well as professional development. The organizations behind the six reforms run the gamut from educational institutions, through foundations and other types of nonprofits, to combinations of the above. The following sections describe each reform effort, presented in order of prevalence, and identify the sponsor of each reform.

Different Ways of Knowing

DWOK was established in 1989 under the auspices of the Galef Foundation, a nonprofit educational organization that aims to improve student achievement through collaboration with public school educators, schools of education, and other educational reform agencies. (See Table 9.1.)

DWOK focuses on improving classroom practices as a means of raising student achievement. Customized to each school and district, DWOK is distinctive in its standards-based interdisciplinary curriculum, which combines literacy and art (including visual, performing and media arts) to help students learn mathematics, social studies, science, reading, and writing. The curriculum is designed to capitalize on multiple intelligences and emphasizes exploration, active student participation, and collaborative learning. Units are organized around three aspects that follow the natural cycle of learning: Coming to Know, Showing You Know, and Knowing You Know.

Coming to Know occurs at the beginning of a unit; in Coming to Know, teachers evaluate students' prior learning history about a particular topic so that they can assess students' strengths and weaknesses. This allows teachers to make informed decisions about the areas in which students are likely to need more help and to design instruction that builds on students' prior experiences. In Showing You Know, teachers have students engage in a variety of activities that demonstrate what they have learned. These activities emphasize innovative modes of learning, particularly the arts, and encourage students to express themselves using both linguistic and non-linguistic forms. In Knowing You Know, teachers help students reflect on and apply their knowledge.

Teachers attend summer institutes and professional development workshops, at which they receive training in thematic, inquiry-based teaching strategies and in

Table 9.1
Different Ways of Knowing

Goals	Key Elements	Services and Support
Raise student achievement Improve students' attitudes toward schools	Standards-based curriculum, instruction, and assessment planning linked to big ideas Learner-centered, inquiry-based instruction Literacy: reading, writing, listening, and speaking all day long Safe, supportive, and well-managed learning environment Visual, performing, literary, and media arts inside the natural cycle of learning Family and community cultures embedded in classroom and school life School is a learning community	On-site coaching by interdisciplinary support team Summer institutes Professional development workshops Leadership institutes for principals and teacher leaders Publications and technology

SOURCE: The program Web site (http://www.dwoknet.galef.org).
NOTE: According to the National Forum to Accelerate Middle School Reforms (2003), this program was being used in 650 elementary and middle schools as of September 2002.

planning "backwards" from standards and assessments. A team consisting of an instructional coach, a leadership coach, and an artist coach provide on-site coaching. These coaches provide professional development to teachers and facilitate study groups. Additionally, principals attend institutes to build their capacity to support teachers, and parents are encouraged to attend workshops and orientations.

Evaluations of DWOK have reported positive results. Catterall (1995) followed 1,000 children over three years and found that greater exposure to DWOK was associated with greater gains. Students with one year of DWOK exposure showed gains of 8 percentage points in language arts achievement, and those with two years of exposure gained approximately 16 percentage points. Non-DWOK students, on the other hand, showed no such changes in scores. During these three years, DWOK students also showed increased motivation and engagement, but non-DWOK students reported a decline in motivation. Other studies have confirmed these results and attest to the capability of the model as a means of improving student outcomes (Peterson et al., 1998; Petrosko, 1997).

Turning Points Transforming Middle Schools Model

Turning Points was originally sponsored by the Carnegie Corporation and is aligned with the recommendations presented in Carnegie Council on Adolescent Development (1989). (See Table 9.2.) The network of Turning Points schools is overseen by

Table 9.2
Turning Points Transforming Middle Schools Model

Goals	Key Elements	Services and Support
Teach a curriculum grounded in standards	Improve learning, teaching, and assessment for all students	On-site coaching
Use instructional methods designed to prepare all students	Build leadership capacity and a professional collaborative cul-ture	Professional development and networking
Prepare teachers for middle grades	Data-based inquiry and deci-sionmaking	Turning Points conferences and institutes
Organize relationships for learn-ing	Create a school culture to sup-port high achievement and personal development	Turning Points self-study
Govern democratically by all staff members	Network with like-minded schools	Publications and technology
Provide a safe and healthy school environment	Develop district capacity to sup-port school change	Accountability and assessments of student learning
	Involve parents and communities in supporting learning	

SOURCE: The program Web site (http://www.turningpts.org).
NOTE: According to the National Forum to Accelerate Middle School Reforms (2003), this program was being used in over 54 schools in 7 states as of September 2002.

the Center for Collaborative Education, which states that it promotes collaborative learning in a supportive environment.

Turning Points is a comprehensive school reform effort that includes six rec-ommended practices organized around seven principles. The model aims for change on a variety of levels, ranging from course content (such as developing an interdisci-plinary curriculum) to relationships between schools and their districts. It recom-mends certain pedagogical practices, including differentiated curricula through flexi-ble grouping of students, authentic assessments,[3] and cooperative learning groups. A key feature of the model involves strengthening teacher-student bonds through the creation of small learning communities and advisory programs. Turning Points schools are also encouraged to engage in a supportive network, not only with other like-minded schools but also with the community at large.

Turning Points includes school visits from coaches who assist the internal facili-tator (appointed by the school) with teacher team meetings and other administrative or instructional issues that arise. There are also conferences and institutes, at which teachers from different schools can share their experiences and insights. Schools are encouraged to develop a strong local network, particularly within their district, to build capacity to sustain changes. Teachers and other staff use data from the Turning Points Self-Survey, which provide information on a variety of areas including teach-

---

[3] Also known as *alternative* or *performance* assessments, these include journals, skits and plays, videos, sur-veys, posters, newspapers, labeled models, timelines, and debates. Authentic methods require students to construct a response based on their independent work, make meaning out of their new knowledge, and put their new skills into action. Source: http://www.middleweb.com/MWLresources/tp2000excrpt.

ing, learning, assessment, teaming, leadership, climate, and student behavior, to evaluate progress.

Evaluations of Turning Points have found improvements in students' standardized test scores. DePascale (1997) reported on 26 middle schools that had implemented the Turning Points principles and found that students in these schools were taking algebra at a significantly higher rate than the state average. Likewise, Felner et al. (1997) found that schools that had implemented the Turning Points recommendations to a high degree had significantly higher achievement scores in mathematics, language, and reading than the overall state average. In addition, decreases in behavior problems and emotional difficulties were also documented. However, simple comparisons to state norms overlook the fact that the sample schools may not be demographically similar to the state as a whole. Overall, Turning Points has shown promise as a means of raising student achievement and decreasing social-emotional problems of middle school students, although it is unclear whether the positive results would be observed on a wider scale.

Making Middle Grades Work

Making Middle Grades Work (MMGW) is sponsored by the Southern Regional Education Board (SREB), an interstate compact that advises leaders in 16 states on educational issues. SREB has done a number of studies of middle school issues, although that is not its sole focus. (See Table 9.3.)

MMGW is a network of schools, districts, and states that aims to improve middle school achievement by changing the content of core academic subjects, the relationships between teachers and students, the support system for teachers, and their teaching practices (SREB, 2002). The model includes a comprehensive improvement framework that lists ten elements and five conditions that are necessary to support changes in climate, practices, and staff. MMGW has a diverse set of features and goals. It emphasizes rigorous standards that clearly specify the kinds of skills and knowledge that students should master to succeed in college-preparatory courses. It also calls for improvements in teacher qualifications, through a state certification process that requires teachers to have more experience with adolescents and more coursework in academic disciplines. The program also encourages school boards to hire teachers whose content specialization matches their teaching assignments (specifically recruiting teachers with subject-specific majors or minors in the subjects they teach). Additionally, MMGW supports alternative scheduling formats to promote interdisciplinary activities and transition or advisory programs to identify students who might need remediation.

Table 9.3
Making Middle Grades Work

Goals	Key Elements	Services and Support
Increase the percentages of 8th graders who perform at the proficient levels in academic subjects Provide educational experiences that increase students' knowledge and skills in reading, mathematics, language arts, science, and social studies Provide students with opportunities to apply their skills in the fine arts and to explore careers and new technology	Academic core that is aligned to what students must know, understand, and be able to do to succeed in college-preparatory English, mathematics, and science A belief that all students matter High expectations and a system of extra help and time Classroom practices that engage students in their learning Teachers working together Support from parents Qualified teachers Use of data Use of technology for learning Strong leadership Essential conditions for raising student achievement Commitment by state partners, local school board, district leaders, and the community Planning for continuous improvement Curriculum aligned to state, national, and international standards Support for professional development Teacher preparation	Site development workshops Three-day technical assistance visit to each school, and subsequent one-day technical review visit Consultation and technical assistance Professional development assistance Research briefs, publications, and other forms of information dissemination Technology-based network and support system (e.g., list-servers, Web pages, etc.) Evaluation of school's progress through the Middle Grades Assessment, which consists of surveys, achievement tests, and data profiles

SOURCE: The program Web site (http://www.sreb.org/programs/MiddleGrades/MiddleGradesindex.asp).
NOTE: According to the National Forum to Accelerate Middle School Reforms (2003), this program was being used in 46 schools in 14 states as of September 2002.

MMGW supports schools through workshops, school visits, research briefs, and technology-based network systems. It administers the Middle Grades Assessment, which consists of principal and teacher surveys, achievement tests, and data profiles that provide demographic and organizational information about the school. The results of this assessment are used to evaluate schools' progress toward the comprehensive improvement framework.

In an external evaluation of MMGW, the Research Triangle Institute collected baseline data on a variety of measures from 24 MMGW schools and again two years later, then compared the results. The evaluators reported generally positive results over the two-year period, including an increase in teachers' reliance on certain practices (e.g., encouraging students to use mathematics in solving real-world problems) and statistically significant achievement gains in reading and mathematics. However, since there was no control group, it is not clear how these effects should be interpreted. They could conceivably be attributed to factors other than the reform model itself (e.g., changes in state or federal educational initiatives during the two-year period). Furthermore, some of the statistically significant results may have been driven by large sample sizes.[4] Thus, MMGW has shown some potential for improving student achievement, but it remains to be seen how much effect the model can have.

Middle Start Initiative

The Middle Start Initiative (Middle Start) is the result of a collaboration between the Academy for Education Development (AED); the W.K. Kellogg Foundation; the Center for Prevention Research and Development at the University of Illinois; and some other, smaller organizations and agencies based in Michigan. Like the other sponsoring groups, AED has a broader mission, working in several areas, including education, youth development, health, and the environment, to solve critical social problems both domestically and abroad. (See Table 9.4.)

Middle Start hopes to improve middle-grade students' achievement and school experiences through a combination of methods. The program endorses creation of small learning communities, fostering collective responsibility for student success, professional development of teachers, and parent and community involvement. Small learning communities are facilitated mainly through interdisciplinary teams and advisory programs, while collective responsibility is promoted through staff decision-making and shared norms about the missions of the school. Middle Start schools are also developing family and community involvement strategies and network activities that allow teachers to exchange ideas, practices, and approaches to teaching.

Middle Start's primary research and evaluation tool is a self-study survey that assesses outcomes in areas ranging from classroom practices to school environment. The program offers leadership workshops and other networking conferences and on-site coaching and technical assistance in a variety of areas, including professional development. Additionally, Middle Start facilitates the establishment of regional networks among service agencies, universities, advocacy groups, and participating schools to foster conditions that uphold school improvement.

As noted in Chapter Three, Middle Start evaluations have found a positive association between implementation and student achievement. However, implementation level was conflated with school demographics. One measure of implementation

---

[4]For example, the difference in achievement over the two years was 2 to 3 points on a scale of more than 150, which is not only well within measurement error but also suggests extremely small gains. Analogously, the changes teachers reported in the activities they chose to use were equally small. In some cases, mean differences in the frequency of promoted practices increased by as little as 0.2 points on a 5-point scale.

Table 9.4
Middle Start Initiative

Goals	Key Elements	Services and Support
Attend to the educational needs of middle grade students, particularly those at risk for low academic achievement Encourage change in policies, practices, and public awareness at the school, district, and state levels to improve teaching and learning Foster school collaboration with other community agencies to provide services to vulnerable students and their families Increase and sustain school attention to curricular areas, especially in reading and mathematics	Reflective review and self-study Small learning communities and a teaming structure Rigorous curriculum, instruction, and student assessment Distributed leadership and sustainable partnerships	On-site coaching Professional development Local network of institutional support stemming from regional partnerships of agencies, universities, and advocacy groups Ongoing leadership workshops and school networking conferences

SOURCE: The program Web site (http://www.middlestart.org).
NOTE: According to the National Forum to Accelerate Middle School Reforms (2003), this program was being used in 41 schools as of September 2002.

level is the time allotted for common planning for team teaching; schools with higher-implementation levels allow more than do schools with lower implementation levels. Lower-implementation schools were more likely to have a larger population of poor students than did higher implementation schools. Specifically, only 8 percent of very poor schools—those at which more than 60 percent of the students are eligible for free or reduced-price lunches—were designated as high-implementation schools. Although Middle Start reported that high-poverty, high-implementing schools showed more gains on the statewide achievement test than did the more-affluent, lower-implementing schools, there were only three high-poverty, high-implementing schools. Hence, it is unclear how generalizable the results are across schools serving large numbers of poor students. Taken together, Middle Start shows promising but tentative effects on student achievement across different types of schools.

Talent Development Middle School Model

TDMS is associated with Johns Hopkins' Center for Social Organization of Schools, an educational research and development center devoted to improving education by developing curricula and providing technical assistance and other forms of support. (See Table 9.5.)

TDMS schools implement research-based instructional programs in reading and language arts, mathematics, science, and U.S. history. The programs are designed to

Table 9.5
Talent Development Middle School Model

Goals	Key Elements	Services and Support
Provide all students the opportunities and supports needed to achieve at world-class levels Provide all teachers with the training and support needed to deliver standards-based instruction Have every 8th grader able to study algebra, read and analyze literature, perform hands-on science experiments, and interpret original documents from history	Research-based instructional programs in each major subject area Focused and sustained subject and grade-specific professional development In-class implementation assistance from curriculum coaches Replacement courses in mathematics and reading Extra-help elective Innovative approaches to school organization High-Five Climate Programs which creates orderly and supportive learning environments	Ongoing subject and grade-specific staff development (30–38 hours per year per subject) Nonevaluative in-classroom implementation assistance provided by a curriculum coach Intensive training in the instructional programs for lead teachers Instructional facilitators who work closely with curriculum coaches, lead teachers and principals to design staff development, customize the instructional programs, and keep the instructional intervention on track

SOURCE: The program Web site (http://www.csos.jhu.edu/tdms).
NOTE: According to the National Forum to Accelerate Middle School Reforms (2003), this program was being used in 23 schools in 7 states as of September 2002.

develop both foundational skills and the advanced reasoning and comprehension skills necessary for success in college preparatory courses. A key element of the model is its emphasis on hands-on, investigative teaching strategies. The model also includes a remedial component, in which students can elect to receive an extra 10 to 12 weeks of instruction in mathematics and reading a year. TDMS schools often use small learning communities, semidepartmentalization, and extended periods for core subjects to facilitate closer teacher-student relationships.

Support from TDMS takes the form of professional development to help teachers implement the instructional programs. Teachers receive 30 to 38 hours of professional development per subject per year for at least two years. During these sessions, teachers learn about subject matter, pedagogical strategies, and classroom management techniques. They also receive in-classroom implementation assistance from curriculum coaches and feedback from lead teachers who have received intensive training in the instructional programs.

Evaluations of TDMS have reported impressive results. MacIver, Plank, and Balfanz (1997) reported an effect size of 0.51 in reading, favoring students enrolled in a TDMS school relative to their peers from matched non-TDMS schools.[5] Similar magnitudes of gains were found in mathematics (Balfanz, MacIver, and Ryan, 1999).

---

[5] As explained in Chapter Four, an effect size is the standardized mean differences between two groups. In educational interventions, effect sizes tend to be small to moderate. For comparison, the effect size for the reduced class size initiative in Tennessee was approximately 0.25 (Finn and Achilles, 1999). The effect sizes shown by TDMS are markedly larger.

In another study, the number of years that students were exposed to TDMS was a significant predictor of students' gains in science achievement, with those who had been exposed to the full version of TDMS experiencing an effect size gain of 0.60 from 4th grade to 7th grade (MacIver, Ruby, et al., 2003). This gain was significantly greater than that shown by students in the matched control school. These findings underscore the potential that TDMS holds for enhancing student learning.

AIM at Middle Grades Results

The Education Development Center, Inc., in partnership with Abt Associates, is responsible for AIM at Middle Grades Results (AIM). (See Table 9.6.) The Education Development Center is a nonprofit organization "dedicated to enhancing learning, promoting health, and fostering a deeper understanding of the world" with over 300 projects around the world. It accomplishes these goals not only by supporting children and families and promoting schools but also by promoting health, building communities, and integrating work and learning.

The AIM model is based on principles that the National Forum to Accelerate Middle Grades Reform has set forth: AIM's mission is to create academically excellent schools that are developmentally responsive to adolescents' needs. The program has six key design features, including a rigorous curriculum and a safe and healthy climate. One distinctive feature is the Teaching for Understanding framework, which provides guidelines for developing coherent curriculum, instruction, and assessments that are aligned with state and local standards. To promote a personalized environment, AIM schools use such practices as clusters or houses, advisory programs, and looping (keeping students together with the same teachers for more than one year). Additionally, participating AIM schools establish links to community groups, such as youth organizations, social-services agencies, and local businesses and industries.

Because AIM focuses on capacity-building, it provides much of its organizational support on site. In addition to providing a site developer who acts as a coach, AIM encourages the development of school leadership teams, which consist of teachers, parents, and community members working together to create conditions that facilitate change. AIM also establishes faculty inquiry teams, whose responsibilities include evaluating progress and identifying areas for improvement, and critical friends coaches, who support the faculty inquiry teams and provide an environment in which individuals can present their concerns and receive feedback.

Very little is known about the effectiveness of the AIM model. To date, most of the research promoting AIM has focused on the research base supporting its design. However, there is indirect evidence for its potential effectiveness. AIM builds on Authentic Teaching, Learning, and Assessment for All Students (ATLAS), a K–12

Table 9.6
AIM at Middle Grades Results

Goals	Key Elements	Services and Support
Provide every student with high quality teachers, resources, learning opportunities, and supports Build strong learning communities to improve student performance Create high-performing middle grade schools that are academically excellent and responsive to developmental needs of adolescents	Rigorous and developmentally responsive curriculum, instruction, and assessment Safe and healthy climate Strong links between family, school, and community Collaborative leadership Ongoing professional development Innovative use and integration of technology	On-site coaching School leadership team, parents, and community members Faculty Inquiry Teams Training to develop Critical Friends Coaches

SOURCE: The program Web site (http://www.takingaim.org).
NOTE: According to the National Forum to Accelerate Middle School Reforms (2003), this program was being used in 8 schools in 5 states as of September 2002).

reform model that emphasizes authentic curriculum and instruction, and the development of coherent educational programs for every student. In citing evidence for the value of AIM, organizations endorsing AIM refer to positive evaluations based on ATLAS schools. Although AIM and ATLAS share many characteristics and goals, they are not identical models. Therefore, it is uncertain whether the positive effects obtained from evaluations of ATLAS can be attributed to the components AIM shares. Thus, there is currently indirect evidence suggesting that AIM can improve student learning, but its full effects remain unknown.

Implementation and Sustainability Issues

In spite of the promising results of many of the current middle school reform models, there is little evidence to suggest whether the effects are sustainable after the initial implementation phase when supports are no longer available. Relying on prior studies, Williamson and Johnston (1999, p. 13) describe the progression of reforms as follows:

> [F]ollowing an initial flurry of activity, . . . teachers met as teams but talked only about student problems. In subsequent years teams met less frequently. One or two interdisciplinary units were arranged and offered a pleasant respite from the "real curriculum." Blocks of time were offered but classes continued to meet forty-five or fifty minutes daily. The curriculum remained basically unchanged.

Other investigations have come to similar conclusions (for example, Braddock, 1990; Lounsbury and Johnston, 1988), suggesting that, despite reform efforts, many middle schools resemble the very schools (that is, the junior highs) they were supposed to reform.

Although the federal government's CSR effort supports the reforms reviewed in this chapter, the schools implementing them will undoubtedly face challenges sooner or later. Bodilly and colleagues (Berends, Bodilly, and Kirby, 2002; Kirby, Berends, and Naftel, 2001) have identified multiple characteristics that are important for implementation and scale-up, including the following:

- **School climate and leadership:** Schools in which faculty and staff experienced fewer conflicts were more likely to successfully implement a model, as were schools with consistent leadership.
- **Informed decisionmaking:** Schools that were well informed about different models and allowed to choose a design implemented the reform more quickly than did schools that were ill informed or not given a choice.
- **Design team:** Schools implemented models to a higher level of fidelity when they collaborated with design teams that showed stable leadership, developed the capacity of teachers, and worked with districts to acquire resources for implementation.
- **District support:** Greater implementation was associated with districts that showed consistent leadership, were devoid of political crises (for example, significant budget reductions), had a history of collaboration between the central office and the schools, provided schools with enough autonomy to implement the model, and provided resources for professional development.

Implementation problems are of particular concern for program developers because research has suggested that low implementation not only prevents the full benefits of the models from being realized but can also be associated with poorer student outcomes (Felner et al., 1997; Mitman, Lash, and Mergendeller, 1985). However, it is important to keep in mind that, even when schools have the benefit of resources and support, reforms do not necessarily lead to better educational outcomes for students (Mackinnon, 2003).

It is also important to keep in mind that many comprehensive reforms may affect students' psychological and social outcomes more than their academic achievement. For example, a study of 23 middle schools implementing practices consistent with the Comer School Development Program (not reviewed here), which emphasizes both the social and cognitive development of students, showed that students' well-being, absenteeism, and involvement with petty misbehaviors, but not their achievement, improved (Cook et al., 1999). Thus, it is critical to continue to examine a wide variety of outcomes of reform models. Appendix D provides examples of process-focused evaluation studies that incorporate both social-motivational and academic measures.

Challenges, Recommendations, and Exploratory Ideas

A distinguishing characteristic of the models this chapter profiles is that they reflect the middle school concept (see Chapter Three). Interdisciplinary team teaching, flexible scheduling, and advisory programs are core features of many of the models. DWOK incorporates interdisciplinary teaching into its design, as do Middle Start and Turning Points. Flexible scheduling is a key element of Making Middle Grades Work, TDMS, and Turning Points. The AIM, Middle Start, and Making Middle Grades Work designs include advisory programs. Additionally, there are other efforts to make schools more developmentally appropriate, ranging from smaller communities and looping to investigative teaching strategies.

Comprehensive school reform models are a promising strategy for improving student achievement both at the middle school level and at other levels of schooling. These programs have several advantages over past reform efforts, especially with respect to coherence (for example, with all facets of school being aligned to the same goal), funding, and teacher support. Some of the reforms require the backing of 80 percent of the staff, thereby reducing the potential contribution of lack of teacher motivation to implementation problems. It is too early to draw definitive conclusions about the effectiveness of all the models or about their potential to be scaled up. However, such reforms as these have the promise to ease many of the challenges middle schools face nationwide.

Although this chapter has profiled some of the specific reform models that are being pursued to improve middle schools, it is important to keep in mind the many other resources for middle schools that we do not address here. For example, we did not discuss other reform-minded groups (such as the Edna McConnell Clark Foundation), which support middle school reform but do not espouse a single model. Similarly, we have not touched upon private philanthropic organizations (such as Grantmakers for Education) and their role in helping to strengthen middle schools' capacity to improve educational outcomes for students. There are other resources that we exclude, such as Middle Web, a Web site that is a valuable source for reform-related news and that includes links to research and articles. We recommend these resources to readers who are interested in learning more about middle school issues more generally.

CHAPTER TEN

Conclusions and Recommendations

In this monograph, we have attempted to integrate data and research on various aspects of middle schools to paint a comprehensive picture of teaching and learning in these schools. This final chapter provides a broader evaluation of the state of the American middle school in light of our review.

As we have indicated throughout our review, there are topics that remain to be explored and types of research that could help answer many important questions and provide additional guidance to policymakers and practitioners. Lack of research on some middle school topics and the absence of certain types of studies limited our analyses and our ability to make recommendations. We therefore provide examples of the types of studies that could add to current and future improvement efforts in Appendix D.

Summary of Findings

The middle school concept, as it has been endorsed since the 1980s, represents an attempt to reform the traditional junior high school structure to create an educational experience more appropriate for young adolescents. The goal was to make the old junior high more developmentally responsive by initially changing the grade configuration, then changing the organizational and instructional practices (for example, by teaming students into smaller units and adding advisory programs). The question now, 20 years after the concept emerged, is how successful middle school reform has been in advancing the academic and developmental growth of our students.

The middle school concept has successfully taken hold, if numbers of middle schools (grades 6–8) as opposed to other structures is any indication. It is now the predominant form of school structure for the early teen years. And our review of the literature made it clear that middle schools have generated tremendous interest from committed educators, innovative reformers, and private foundations. This level of interest and activity is impressive and, in and of itself, suggests that the middle grades are not the wasteland of U.S. education that the media has suggested. Collaborative networks, such as the National Forum to Accelerate Middle Grades Reform, provide middle-grade educators, advocates, reformers, foundation representatives, and researchers a forum in which to discuss ways to improve middle school education. They are excellent examples of the commitment and good will that can help the field move forward.

But significant issues remain if the middle school concept is to do a better job than the old junior high structure did at meeting teens' developmental needs and propelling academic achievement. At least on the surface, many of these issues appear to be highly interrelated. For example, poor academic outcomes are associated with negative school climates and disciplinary problems. They can also be associated with the lack of strong teacher subject-matter expertise that we found in the middle grades. The main challenges discussed in this report are summarized below.

Separating the Middle Grades Is Scientifically Unsound

Our history of reform (Chapter Two) indicated that the scientific rationale for creating separate schools for young adolescents was weak. Middle schools have become the norm more because of social and demographic pressures than because of scientific evidence supporting the need for a separate school for young teens. Not only is evidence showing that young teens benefit from a separate three years of schooling weak, there is strong evidence suggesting that transitions (especially if they involve several changes in the school environment and instruction) have at least temporarily negative effects on some youth. Separate elementary schools and middle schools cause transition problems for students that can negatively affect their developmental and academic progress. In short, the research findings indicate that the separate middle school has weak empirical support.

Progress on Academic Outcomes Is Positive but Uneven

Important improvements in academic achievement for the middle grades have been documented. For example, NAEP data show slow, but steady, increases in achievement scores since the 1970s (see Chapter Four). This general positive trend, however, masks some very troubling and persistent shortfalls in the improvement of students' academic performance.

The majority of U.S. 8th graders in public schools—about 70 percent (see Chapter Four)—fail to reach proficient levels of performance in reading, mathematics, and science on national achievement tests.

Our analyses also reveal that the greatest challenge lies in improving learning for African-American and Latino students and for children of parents who did not finish high school. Middle school students from economically disadvantaged groups and from ethnic and racial minorities continue to lag behind their peers in academic achievement. Disparities among different demographic groups are not unique to middle schools, but they nevertheless remain a major challenge, inasmuch as such group differences are more likely to increase than decrease, or have potentially more-negative consequences, during the middle grades.

Conditions for Learning in Middle Schools Are Suboptimal

Although middle schools were created to address the emotional and social developmental needs of early teens, middle school students report suboptimal conditions for learning. Our analyses of international data in Chapter Five showed that, compared to similar-age peers in 11 other Western nations, U.S. students of middle school age report the highest levels of physical and emotional problems. They also view the climates and peer cultures in their schools more negatively.

Middle schools have disciplinary problems that affect students and teachers and increase the workload of principals. Poor academic performance is related to discipline problems, and national school safety statistics suggest that physical conflict and bullying are especially problematic in middle schools. Public middle school teachers report getting physically threatened by students. As we discussed in Chapter Six, the need to deal with disciplinary issues increases a principal's workload and can decrease the time and effort spent on other leadership functions (for example, providing instructional supports). Yet school safety is rarely explicitly discussed in the middle school literature.

The Vision of the Middle School Has Not Been Fully Implemented

The continuing lackluster performance of middle schools might also be explained, in part, by another of our findings: The implementation of the middle school concept has been less than adequate in most districts and schools (for example, Felner, Jackson, et al., 1997; Williamson and Johnston, 1999). Although some of the core practices, such as interdisciplinary team teaching and advisory programs, are found in middle schools, our reviews in Chapters Three and Nine indicated that they tend to be implemented weakly, with little attention to the underlying goals. Therefore, the current level of implementation has not helped schools achieve the goals that the practices were designed to reach. Furthermore, there is some evidence that poorly and inadequately implemented practices have negative effects (for example, achievement losses and increased behavior problems; see Felner et al. 1987 and Mitman, Lash, and Mergendeller, 1985). We conclude that, at the national level, the middle school reform has not been implemented as conceived. It is reasonable to assume that a sufficient level of fidelity to many of the reform practices is not possible without substantial additional attention, resources, and support over the long run.

Evaluation of Success Focuses Too Narrowly on Achievement

Research most often assesses the effectiveness of the middle school practices by examining student academic outcomes. For example, the available data from evaluations of specific reform models indicate that the models show promise for raising standardized test scores. However, little research has been published on other indicators, such as student engagement, aspirations, school climate, or disciplinary issues.

Because most of the practices promoted as part of middle school reform since the 1980s were designed to facilitate developmental responsiveness, not necessarily academic outcomes, it is not clear whether it is appropriate to use academic achievement as the sole indicator of the practices' effectiveness. Teaming practices, for example, were designed to lessen student anonymity and to facilitate closer student-teacher connections; their effectiveness could be assessed by relying on indicators of school climate. The effects of interdisciplinary team teaching, in turn, should include measures of student motivation, as well as academic achievement.

We conclude that the middle school concept's focus on problems other than achievement is well warranted. However, we also conclude that the evidence on the positive effects of the middle school concept on a national scale is weak. *Weak* here refers both to a lack of studies and to the fact that some of the evidence relies on studies with limited generalizability. In particular, there is a dearth of studies that examine how middle school reforms may first raise student motivation, improve school climate, or decrease disciplinary problems and how such changes in turn might be related to achievement over time.

Middle School Teachers and Principals Lack Appropriate Training and Support

The less-than-optimal conditions for teaching and learning and the inadequate level of implementation of promising practices in middle schools might also be associated with the fact that many middle school teachers lack knowledge about their main subject areas and about developmentally responsive instructional and classroom management methods. Many who teach English, mathematics, and science in middle schools lack a major, minor, or certification in these subjects. In fact, middle school students are more likely to have a qualified gym teacher than a trained math instructor. In addition, only 25 percent of middle school teachers report having specialized middle-level professional preparation (McEwin, Dickinson, and Swaim, 1996). If middle schools increase their efforts to recruit from nontraditional pools, it is even less likely that teachers will have had formal training in the development of young adolescents. Although it is unclear what type of developmental training will most benefit teachers, training in classroom management skills appropriate to young teens might be of benefit.

Similar training issues are likely to apply to principals. Most important, however, principals of middle schools (especially large ones) may compromise instructional leadership for the sake of operational management. Different management approaches need to be considered that allow principals to delegate multiple managerial duties, yielding the opportunity to foster a strong instructional vision and a climate that is conducive for teaching and learning.

Parental Support Wanes in the Middle Years

Middle schools are not helping parents stay involved with the school lives of their children. Research shows that parental involvement declines as students progress through grade levels. However, our review also showed that middle schools do less than elementary schools do to engage parents. When trying to engage parents, it is also important to consider which forms of involvement are feasible for parents and helpful for students.

New Reform Models Show Promise

Our review of whole-school reforms and our more-limited review of professional development practices indicate that some promising models exist that, if fully implemented, might propel schools toward the high levels of achievement that NCLB requires. Most whole-school reform models that cover the early teen years address both academic achievement and the development needs of early teens. For example, AIM and Turning Points identify improving school climate and student health among their primary goals. In addition, they attempt to address issues of teacher subject-matter expertise and low parental involvement. These models provide examples of promising practices that could be adopted to improve the current schools. In addition, information from other countries, where students view their schools more favorably and feel emotionally and physically healthier, could be better utilized.

Recommendations

The recommendations and exploratory ideas below are intended to provide some practical ideas for improving education for young teens, but they are neither extensive nor detailed. Unlike other recent reports on middle schools (for example, Jackson and Davis, 2000), the goal of our review was to provide a global assessment of the current state of affairs not to develop highly specific recommendations.

Over the coming years, states and school districts might consider alternative structures that allow them to reduce multiple transitions across grades K–12 and facilitate alignment of goals, curriculum, and instructional and organizational approaches across three separate levels of schooling (middle, elementary, and high schools). We propose this as a long-range goal, not as an immediate next step. Capitalizing on continuity of schooling and introducing changes gradually (for example, increasing the number of specialized teachers with in-depth subject-matter expertise earlier than 6th grade) might not only serve students better, it might also provide more flexibility in hiring practices for districts. A school structure with more than a few grade levels might also increase the accountability of schools trying to address problems (for example, achievement gaps between certain demographic groups) before they escalate.

The greatest improvement efforts should now focus on the lowest-performing students by relying on promising practices to facilitate learning without compromising student motivation. To reduce the differences between certain demographic groups, there also need to be greater efforts to address early signs of achievement problems in elementary schools. Although research on the best (proven) practices for middle schools is lacking, there is substantial agreement on the school characteristics and promising practices that facilitate learning. For example, schools fostering both a strong work ethic and a sense of support promote student achievement and other forms of adaptive functioning. Offering different compensatory programs before and after 6th grade can improve the performance of the lowest-performing students. For example, the Talent Development Model provides elective reading and mathematics courses for the lowest-achieving students during the middle grades. The latest findings from research beyond the middle grades offer other alternatives. Modified school calendars and summer programs need to be further explored, inasmuch as some of the learning losses among economically disadvantaged students appear to take place during summer months. Given the somewhat limited knowledge base, it appears worth experimenting with summer programs for the lowest-performing students *before* they reach 6th grade and by offering additional reading and mathematics courses after 6th grade.

We also know what does not work. The research Chapter Five reviewed shows that grade retention is not a productive strategy for promoting achievement or motivation. Grade retention during middle school is one of the strongest predictors of dropping out. Strict promotion policies and increased retention rates can have detrimental consequences on subsequent dropout rates.

Principals and teachers of early teens need to adopt comprehensive prevention models (for example, schoolwide antibullying programs) that focus on changing the social norms or the peer culture that fosters antisocial behavior. Increased control in the form of zero-tolerance policies is not the answer, inasmuch as such strategies appear to further distance and alienate youth from school. Rather than expecting each school to start from scratch, several professional organizations provide helpful advice via their Web sites. In addition, principals are likely to benefit from on-site technical assistance and from professional networks that help them adopt and administer more-effective school discipline approaches (see Chapter Six).

Evidence-based models of professional development should be adopted to compensate for the lack of preservice training for middle school teachers. Although many middle school reforms advocate separate credentials for middle school teachers, we do not recommend requiring special certification at this time. Given the available information, it is not clear that middle school teacher-education programs can make a greater difference in student performance, motivation, and discipline than well-implemented professional development of the existing teacher force. However, professional development appears to need considerable improvement. As Chapter Seven suggests, effective professional development is ongoing, systematic, and closely related to the daily work of teachers. It allows teachers to collaborate, experiment, and reflect.

Middle-grade administrators and teachers should provide information about school practices and offer concrete suggestions for activities that parents and their young teens can do together at home. In addition, we encourage schools to provide workshops for parents about developmental issues, perhaps in collaboration with community groups. The research we discussed in Chapter Eight indicates some simple strategies for improving parental support of middle grade students through better information about student needs and the schools' practices and goals. Although the potential usefulness of parent workshops or courses on developmental changes affecting young teens is not known, such efforts should be explored.

A comparative research program should be established to learn from other countries how to best facilitate student well-being and more-positive school climates in a way that supports academic achievement. As Chapters Two and Five suggested, academic goals are often pitted against the goal of fostering the social-emotional well-being of students. Yet these goals need not conflict with one another. Although social-emotional well-being is not sufficient to promote higher academic achievement, physical or emotional problems do compromise student scholarship. Creative combinations of promising middle-grade practices, such as advisory programs (see Chapter Three) that connect teachers and students; comprehensive disciplinary approaches that aim to change the peer-group norms (Chapter Five); and higher academic standards are needed to provide all students better conditions for learning.

Looking to the Future

The low achievement levels of middle school students have received and are likely to receive even more public concern in light of the current accountability movement and of the NCLB mandates in particular. There is a great emphasis now on the need for higher standards (such as those NCLB articulated) and for increased accountability through academic testing.

But this emphasis poses at least two challenges for middle schools. First, one of the great successes of the middle school concept is that it has made it difficult to ignore developmental issues. Developmental responsiveness is now part of the language of the middle grades, although the way the concept has been pitted against other goals, such as academic rigor, might have reduced its appeal. As legislation focused solely on academic achievement outcomes (such as NCLB) holds greater sway, the developmental needs of children might take second place, even though the two are highly interrelated.

Second, it is unclear whether adequate federal and state support is available for the lowest-performing schools or students to help them meet the new high standards.

Regardless of the nature and scope of future middle grade reform efforts, state and federal support is needed now. States can promote flexible organizational formats for the middle grades, encourage instructional strategies that support achievement goals without compromising student motivation, and offer concrete help and assistance to the lowest-performing schools in the forms of school-based professional development and coaching. At the national level, there should be efforts to identify research priorities that advance practice; compare intermediate schooling in other countries to discover alternative approaches to middle school structure, instruction, etc.; and provide support for schools to help them implement effective disciplinary approaches.

During these hard economic times, the efforts of various agencies, organizations, and foundations should be well coordinated to cover the various needs and to prevent the current challenges from escalating. We need to keep in mind that, from developmental, organizational, and educational perspectives, continuity rather than change is likely to provide better conditions for student growth, institutional improvement, and educational progress. Thrashing about from educational fad to educational fad is not likely to pay high dividends. Thus, while NCLB provides a felt need for urgency, that urgency should not be translated into groping, ill-formed efforts at change. It should be translated into steady, reasoned attempts to improve the schooling of all our young teens.

Characteristics of U.S. Public Schools Serving Middle Grades

CCD is a nationally representative statistical database of U.S. public elementary, middle, and secondary schools (NCES, 2000–2001); it is the nation's most comprehensive database of schools and school districts. We used the CCD to examine characteristics of middle schools, make comparisons among schools that serve middle school–aged students but include different grade configurations, and determine whether schools that are configured differently serve different populations of students, for example, students from disadvantaged households. Our methodology is described in more detail in Chapter One.

This appendix first presents the CCD data we used (all for the 2000–2001 school year). Some observations about the data follow.

School Demographics

Table A.1 illustrates the way student enrollment, racial composition, per-pupil teacher ratio, and the percentage of students from disadvantaged households vary by grade configuration (5–8, 6–8, 7–8, K–8, and other) and locale (urban, suburban, rural). Although the most common middle school configurations are 5–8, 6–8, and 7–8, a substantial number (3,170) of these schools had the K–8 configuration, which serves both middle school– and elementary-age students. "All Other Grade Configurations" includes all schools that did not fall into the other categories.

According to NCES, CCD had records available for 96,570 schools, of which 95,366 were open during the 2000–2001 school year. CCD records include schools that were open one year and closed the next; closed schools remain in the CCD database for one year. Of the 95,366 schools, 87,442 are regular elementary and secondary public schools; 2,038 were special education schools; 1,041 were vocational or technical schools; and 4,845 were other or alternative schools. We restricted our analysis to the following:

- schools in regular elementary, middle, and secondary school configurations
- schools that were open during the 2000–2001 school year

Table A.1
Characteristics of U.S. Public Schools (Different Configurations)

Grade Configuration	Schools in Each Locale[a]		Students in Each Locale		Student-Teacher Ratio	Free and Reduced-Price Lunches (%)	African American (%)	Latino (%)
	Number	%	Number	%				
Grades 5–8								
Rural	832	2.3	353,682	2.5	14.5	37.7	7.3	5.6
Suburban	406	1.4	256,541	1.4	14.4	28.7	11.3	9.7
Urban	163	0.8	119,276	0.9	13.1	67.2	40.8	27.5
All locales	1,401	1.6	729,499	1.6				
Grades 6–8								
Rural	3,149	8.6	1,515,321	10.7	15.1	37.4	9.6	7.4
Suburban	3,113	10.9	2,497,181	13.4	16.4	30.2	13.0	13.3
Urban	2,262	11.0	1,828,106	13.6	16.8	55.0	33.4	22.0
All locales	8,524	10.0	5,840,608	12.6				
Grades 7–8								
Rural	1,215	3.3	346,379	2.4	14.7	37.2	5.8	6.6
Suburban	929	3.3	633,758	3.4	16.6	30.2	12.3	14.7
Urban	442	2.1	326,056	2.4	16.2	47.0	20.5	24.7
All locales	2,586	3.0	1,306,193	2.8				
Grades K–8								
Rural	2,029	5.5	443,608	3.1	11.8	39.3	3.2	7.5
Suburban	593	2.1	302,560	1.6	15.6	38.6	12.0	24.0
Urban	548	2.7	319,572	2.4	16.5	51.6	37.9	24.5
All locales	3,170	3.7	1,065,740	2.3				

Table A.1—Continued

Grade Configuration	Schools in Each Locale[a]		Students in Each Locale		Student-Teacher Ratio	Free and Reduced-Price Lunches (%)	African American (%)	Latino (%)
	Number	%	Number	%				
All other grade configurations								
Rural	29,371	80.3	11,488,308	81.2	14.5	39.3	8.1	6.4
Suburban	23,465	82.3	14,972,781	80.2	16.3	31.8	13.2	14.0
Urban	17,150	83.4	10,865,012	80.7	15.5	56.2	32.7	23.1
All locales	69,986	81.7	37,326,101	80.7				
Total								
Rural	36,596		14,147,298					
Suburban	28,506		18,662,821					
Urban	20,565		13,458,022					
All locales	85,667		46,268,141					

[a]Typically, comparisons across locales include examining differences between urban, suburban, and rural areas. The Office of Management and Budget (OMB) designates areas as Central Metropolitan Statistical Areas (CMSAs) and Metropolitan Statistical Areas (MSAs). For CCD, urban areas include both central cities of CMSAs having populations of 250,000 or more and midsize cities with populations less than 250,000. Communities that share strong social and economic ties with a central city or an urbanized core fall within these categories. CMSAs meet the criteria of a population of 1 million persons (for more information, see U.S. Census Bureau, 2003). Suburban areas combine incorporated areas of large and midsize cities of CMSAs or MSAs and large towns, which typically lie outside of a CMSA or MSA. Large towns have populations greater than 25,000. Rural areas can be inside or outside a CMSA or an MSA; the Census Bureau uses certain population-level criteria in making this designation (NCES Documentation, 2000–2001 Common Core). Small towns have populations between 2,500 and 25,000 and are combined with the rural category.

- schools located within the 50 states, the District of Columbia, and certain territories
- Department of Defense schools outside the United States
- schools affiliated with the Bureau of Indian Affairs.

Of the 87,442 operating public elementary and secondary schools, some schools were not coded for locale and therefore are left out of the analysis (see Table A.2).

Nearly 6 million students were enrolled in public middle schools that had the 6–8 configuration. This is by far the most common type of school for young teens. Students in 6–8 schools represented 12.6 percent of all students in K–12 schools; 1.6 percent were in 5–8 schools, 2.8 percent in 7–8 schools, and 2.3 percent in K–8 schools.

Significant Observations

Grade Configuration and Locale

Simply in terms of numbers, most 6–8 schools were in rural areas. However, a higher percentage of all schools in urban areas had this configuration (11 percent) than those in rural areas (9 percent). Although 7–8 schools were more common than 5–8 schools overall, larger proportions of the schools in rural and suburban areas had one of these configurations than did schools in urban areas. In comparison, 6–8 schools were as common in urban areas as they were in rural and suburban areas. Rural areas had a higher proportion of K–8 schools (5.5 percent) than did schools in the suburban (2.1 percent) and urban areas (2.7 percent).

A number of important differences in characteristics exist across the different grade configurations and are discussed individually below.

Student-Teacher Ratios

In suburban (14.4) and urban areas (13.1), 5–8 schools had significantly lower student-teacher ratios than did the other configurations, meaning that these schools have smaller classes. In rural areas, the same is true for K–8 schools (11.8).

Table A.2
Schools Not Coded for Locale

Grade Configuration	Number of Schools	Number of Students
5–8	4	1,920
6–8	21	14,491
7–8	14	7,493
K–8	27	10,196
All other	1,709	711,919

Free and Reduced-Price Lunch

In suburban areas, K–8 schools enroll a disproportionately larger percentage of economically disadvantaged students (38.6 percent) than do other middle school configurations. In urban locales, nontraditional middle schools, such as 5–8 schools, enroll a significantly greater proportion of economically disadvantaged students (67.2 percent) than do the traditional 6–8 schools (55 percent).

African-American Students

In general, urban middle schools of any particular grade configuration tended to have larger populations of African-American students than did the same configurations in rural and suburban schools. Note in particular that the highest percentage of urban African Americans attended 5–8 schools (40.8 percent), and the lowest percentage attended 7–8 schools (20.5 percent). The percentages varied less for rural schools, but those for suburban schools varied the least.

Latino Students

The enrollment of Latino students across different types of middle schools varied most among grade configurations in suburban areas, with few differences between urban and rural areas. Latino enrollments in suburban areas range from a low of 9.7 percent in 5–8 schools to a high of 24 percent in K–8 schools. For all grade configurations except K–8 schools, urban schools enrolled a greater percentage of Latino students than did rural and suburban areas combined. In K–8 schools, suburban and urban areas enrolled equal proportions of Latino students, albeit significantly greater than in rural areas.

International and National Data Sets

Much of the data on middle schools in this report come from (but are not limited to) two international and four U.S. data sets:

- The Third International Math and Science Study (TIMSS) and TIMSS-R
- Health Behavior in School-Aged Children (HBSC)
- Common Core of Data
- The National Assessment of Educational Progress (NAEP)
- The National Education Longitudinal Study of 1988 (NELS:88)
- Schools and Staffing Survey (SASS)

We review findings from studies that have analyzed these data, but we also conducted our own analyses with four of the sets (HBSC, CCD, SASS, and, to a lesser degree, NELS:88). The data sets are described in more detail below.

International Data

The Third International Math and Science Study and Its Repeat

It is important to examine cross-national comparisons of achievement because the academic performance of U.S. students relative to their international peers serves as one indicator of how well U.S. students are really doing and of their ability to compete in a global economy. TIMSS is a cross-national survey of student achievement, curriculum, and instruction in mathematics and science education.[1] First conducted in 1995 with 45 countries, TIMSS sampled students from five grade levels, including the two adjacent grades that contained the largest proportion of 9-year-olds and of 13-year-olds, respectively, at the time of testing. The study also sampled students in

---

[1] While this manuscript was in press, TIMSS, formerly known as the "Third International Mathematics and Science Study" became the "Trends in International Mathematics and Science Study." This change coincided with the public release of the results from the 2003 administration. Because of the timing, we could not incorporate the 2003 results into our analysis. Thus, throughout this manuscript, TIMSS refers to earlier administrations, when the program was still known as the Third International Mathematics and Science Study.

their final year of schooling. This resulted in assessment results from students enrolled in grades 3–4, 7–8, and 12 for most countries.

The study was repeated in 1999 with students from 38 countries. This study, known as TIMSS-R, sampled students who were enrolled in the higher of the two adjacent grades that contained the greatest proportion of 13-year-olds at the time of testing. For the majority of countries, this corresponded to students enrolled in the 8th grade.

School and student sample size varied by nation, but participation rates were generally high, especially for TIMSS-R, for which participation rates exceeded 90 percent for most countries. Overall, the TIMSS sample included nearly 290,000 7th- and 8th-grade students in 6,785 schools, while the TIMSS-R sample contained 180,700 8th-grade students in 6,076 schools (Foy, 1998; Gonzales et al., 2001). Chapter Four describes TIMSS-R findings.

Health Behavior in School-Aged Children

Initiated in 1982, WHO's HBSC study surveys nationally representative samples of 11- to 16-year-olds from 36 countries about their physical, social, and emotional well being. The HBSC surveys for each nation contain a common set of items in four areas: background factors, individual and social resources, health behaviors (such as drug use), and health outcomes (such as somatic complaints). The objectives of HSBC are to monitor trends in adolescents' behaviors and attitudes over time to provide information for health intervention programs and about the context in which attitudes and behaviors develop.

Our analyses for this report focused on school-related questions and indicators of student psychosocial adjustment among 11.5- to 14.5-year-old students, using data collected in 1997 and 1998. We obtained school-relevant data from the HBSC survey for 12 countries that also have TIMSS achievement data. Although we could not directly compare the TIMSS and HBSC data because the targeted populations were not of comparable ages, including both types of data allowed some rough estimates of *relative rankings* among the 12 countries across various indices of adaptive functioning of young teens.

Our main analyses of the HBSC data pertain to scale development because our goal was to identify relevant dimensions of school context and psychosocial adjustment. A factor analysis identified seven reliable dimensions (such as psychological and physical problems, school climate, teacher encouragement, and parental support) that allowed us to compare the U.S. middle school age students to their same-age peers in the other 11 countries. We analyzed data on 32,793 students across the 12 nations and used weights to adjust for differences in populations and subpopulations across nations. See Chapter Five for our findings from the HBSC analyses.

National Data

Common Core of Data

CCD is a nationally representative statistical database of U.S. public elementary, middle, and secondary schools (NCES, 2000–2001). It is the nation's most-comprehensive database on schools and school districts and is based on an annual survey. The data include student body characteristics, geographic locations, school sizes, teacher-pupil ratios, and per-pupil expenditures.

We used CCD to make comparisons across different grade configurations serving U.S. middle school students (5–8, 6–8, and 7–8 schools) to provide the most recent depictions of the middle grades in the United States. We restricted the analysis to include public elementary and secondary schools in operation during the 2000–2001 school year, which yielded data on 87,442 middle schools.

In analyzing CCD, we compared mean differences in the percentages of schools and students served across configurations and across locales (specifically, urban, suburban, and rural areas). Chapter Two discusses the results, and Appendix C provides additional descriptive statistics.

The National Assessment of Educational Progress

NAEP examines the achievement levels of U.S. students in a number of subjects. One component of NAEP, known as *long-term trend NAEP*, assesses basic competency in several subject areas, including mathematics, science, and reading. The primary purpose of long-term trend NAEP is to monitor changes in the progress of 9-, 13-, and 17-year-olds over time. Because the same assessments have been administered periodically since 1969, it is possible to track student achievement back to 1969 in science, 1971 in reading, and 1973 in mathematics across the different age groups.

Another component is *main* NAEP. Its primary objective is to show what students know and can do. Unlike long-term trend NAEP, which has remained substantively unchanged since its inception, the content of main NAEP is flexible enough to adapt to contemporary curricular reforms and changes in assessment approaches. Thus, main NAEP is less amenable than long-term trend NAEP is to tracking changes over considerable periods of time. Main NAEP also differs from long-term trend NAEP in its sampling techniques, using grade-level sampling (i.e., 4th, 8th, and 12th) as opposed to age level sampling (i.e., 9-, 13-, and 17-year-olds). For these reasons, main NAEP and long-term trend NAEP are not comparable measures and are considered different indicators of student achievement. Together, the long-term and main NAEP provide a picture of student achievement from both contemporary and historical perspectives. Chapter Four describes our NAEP findings.

The National Education Longitudinal Study of 1988

NELS:88 data also pertain to student achievement. The data set consists of stratified, nationally representative longitudinal data that followed a sample of 24,599 8th graders as they transitioned to high school and into postsecondary institutions or the labor market. NELS:88 consists of a series of questionnaires for students and their parents, schools, and teachers. It also includes cognitive tests that assess individual status and growth in mathematics; science; reading; and history, geography, and citizenship. The battery of tests was administered at the 8th, 10th, and 12th grades. All the 8th-grade tests consisted solely of multiple-choice items, but in later years, tests in mathematics and science also contained open-ended items.

Because NELS:88 samples were obtained through a complex design (i.e., stratified multistage cluster) and because certain subgroups were oversampled to ensure sufficient representation, it is necessary to take into account the effects of student clustering within schools and the differential probabilities of selection. The results Chapter Four describes are the estimated number of correct scores in mathematics, science, and reading, adjusted for student clustering and unequal selection probabilities. Chapter Eight refers to earlier studies on other topics, such as parental involvement, that used NELS:88 data.

Schools and Staffing Survey

All of the data sets discussed above focus on students. In contrast, the U.S. Department of Education's SASS provides information about a broad variety of topics, including teacher and school demographics, school programs, and general conditions in schools. SASS includes four questionnaires—one each on schools, teachers, principals, and school districts—and collects information from nationally representative U.S. public, private, and charter schools at the elementary, middle, and secondary levels. SASS also assesses information about principals' and teachers' perceptions of school settings, teaching practices, professional development activities, and student demographics.

To complement the student data, we analyzed data from the SASS data collected during the 1999–2000 school year (SASS, 2000). Only respondents in schools that were classified as elementary, middle, or high schools were included. Middle schools were defined as those configured as grades 5–8, 6–8, or 7–8. Elementary schools consisted of K–4, K–5, or K–6 configuration, and high schools consisted of 9–12 or 10–12 configuration. The SASS analyses entailed linear and logistic regressions that controlled for differences in certain school characteristics, such as locale or school ethnic diversity. We also adjusted the standard errors to account for possible correlation among respondents in the same school and used weights to make inferences to the national population.

There were two sources of data. The first source consisted of 7,420 elementary school teachers; 4,527 middle school teachers; and 14,497 high school teachers. Our analyses focused on descriptive data about middle school teachers' professional development and on the differences between their training activities and those for elementary and secondary school teachers. The second source of data was 2,308 elementary school principals, 1,088 middle school principals, and 2,445 high school principals. We analyzed these data to determine how middle school principals spend their time vis-à-vis their goals for their schools and whether the goals or time allocation for certain activities differed from those of principals at other grade levels. Principals (or other administrators serving as their proxies) also answered items about their school program and practices, including the kinds of services offered to facilitate parent involvement and the prevalence of certain practices espoused by middle school advocates (such as teaming). Chapters Six and Seven discuss our findings from the SASS analyses, and Chapters Three and Eight present results from the SASS School Survey.

Factor Analysis of Health Behavior in School-Aged Children

The HBSC survey is an international survey administered to 11-, 13-, and 15-year-olds in different parts of Europe, in North America, and in Israel (WHO, 1997–1998, p. 6).

Our analysis focused on the nations that had participated in TIMSS-R. Table C.1 provides the number of respondents in the samples for each country, as well as for the particular age group that is the focus of this monograph (11.5- to 14.5-year-old students). As the table shows, 1,800 to 3,900 per country fell into our age range. The total number of students included in our analyses was 32,793.

To examine the factors that capture the social-emotional and motivational factors shown to be related to achievement (see Chapter Five), we conducted factor analyses. Factor analysis is used to form constructs that capture clusters or groups of items that are closely related and thus presumed to be tapping a common underlying

Table C.1
HBSC Sample Sizes by Nation and Age Group

	Number of Students	
Nation	In Each National Sample[a]	In Our Study Sample[b]
Belgium	4,824	2,564
Canada	6,567	3,387
Czech Republic	3,703	1,827
England	6,373	3,956
Finland	4,864	2,932
Hungary	3,609	2,679
Israel	5,054	3,312
Latvia	3,775	1,835
Lithuania	4,513	2,583
Russia	3,997	2,184
Slovak Republic	3,789	2,226
United States	5,169	3,308

SOURCE: WHO (1997–1998), p. 9.
[a]Each national sample included 11-, 13-, and 15-year-olds.
[b]We used a subset of the national sample, excluding students who did not fall into the middle school age group (11.5 to 14.5 years old).

construct (Tabachnick and Fidell, 1989). Using the principal-factor extraction method and oblique rotation allowed us to identify factors that are correlated (rather than orthogonal).

Our initial factor analyses yielded an interpretable 10-factor solution, which a Scree test supported. We used a minimum cutoff loading of 0.40 to include items on any particular scale. However, we retained only seven factors, because the remaining three were not robust across different types of exploratory factor analyses. Furthermore, the three factors had low loadings (items were in the low 0.40s), consisted of only two or three items, and had lower internal consistency estimates than did the seven factors we retained. Hence, the analyses here exclude them.[1]

Table C.2 lists the seven factors and includes Cronbach alphas, which are values that depict the internal consistency of the factors. The factors are sorted by strongest to lowest alpha. As the tables show, "school climate" had the largest eigenvalue and proportion of variance explained. The next set of factors explaining the most variance in the data were "psychological and physical problems," followed by "teacher support."

Interfactor Correlations

The interfactor correlations reveal that "school climate" and "teacher support" correlated strongly (r = 0.59). "Physical and psychological problems" and "social alienation" also correlated highly (r = 0.49). "Social alienation" and "peer culture," correlated negatively (r = −0.41).

Standardizing Scores

We standardized items associated with the factors in Table A.3 into z-scores for use in making cross-national comparisons. Computing z-scores allowed us to combine items that were scored using different scales. We had to exclude some student records from our computations because their records lacked information on some items. The z-score computations included population weights (WHO, 1997–1998, pp. 9, 269–270).

---

[1] Specifically, the weak factors we captured were "academic orientation (achievement level and expectations for future)," "delinquency," and "school aversion." In each case, the items were tapping meaningful constructs, but the factor loadings and the internal consistency estimates were not acceptable. With additional items tapping these dimensions, we expect these factors to become more reliable.

Table C.2
Loadings for Seven Factors Retained

Factor	Items	Factor Loading	Alpha	Eigen-value	Proportion of Variance Explained
School climate[a]	Liking school	0.69655			
	School is a nice place	0.67973			
	School is boring[b]	0.64192			
	I belong at school	0.54086			
	School rules are fair	0.43674			
			0.75	5.43	0.53
Physical and psycho-logical problems	Stomachache	0.61252			
	Headache	0.60813			
	Irritable, bad temper	0.60032			
	Nervous	0.56589			
	Feeling low	0.53674			
	Sleeping difficulties	0.41988			
			0.75	2.26	0.22
Teacher support	Teacher gets help when needed	0.62168			
	Teacher interest in me	0.61491			
	Teacher treats mefairly	0.59767			
	Teacher expresses own view	0.53557			
			0.74	1.36	0.13
Peer culture	Students kind and helpful	0.69414			
	Students enjoy being together	0.63973			
	Students accept me	0.49826			
			0.70	0.78	0.08
Social alienation	Left out of things	0.67094			
	Alone at school	0.56067			
	Helpless	0.53656			
	Feel lonely	0.44628			
	Been bullied	0.42163			
			0.68	1.04	0.10
Perceived school pressure	Teacher expects too much	0.65491			
	Parent expects too much	0.64406			
			0.68	0.49	0.04
Parental involvement	Parent comes to school	0.60571			
	Parent ready to help	0.60526			
	Parent encourages to do well	0.57126			
			0.67	0.56	0.05

[a]Note that alpha associated with this factor also includes "taking part in setting rules," not illustrated here because it did not load robustly on the factor in the analysis, although it is a school climate type of construct.
[b]Reverse coded so that the interpretation should be that higher numbers indicate the respondent places less emphasis on being bored at school.

Research Recommendations

This appendix provides some specific examples of types of studies that could further guide reform efforts for the middle grades. Our goal is not to list all the topics that need further study (we have indicated this throughout the chapters) but rather to describe how particular research designs would allow inferences about the direction of effects or how certain statistical tests help us better understand the processes underlying certain effects. We emphasize here also the need to include multiple outcome measures for evaluation research.

Effects of Instructional and Organizational Practices

In Chapter Three, we recommend examining additional indicators of success besides achievement in evaluation studies. Most evaluation research examines the effects of instructional (or organizational) practices on standardized achievement scores. However, if interdisciplinary teaming, flexible scheduling, or advisory programs can positively influence factors other than student achievement, these improvements in and of themselves can justify the implementation of these practices. For example, many of these practices are presumed to make learning more relevant and engaging, yet motivational measures are rarely considered for evaluation purposes. It seems likely that some of the recommended practices that alter the organization of the school day or that facilitate social interaction should have profound effects on students' engagement levels. Although some of the motivational effects might be more immediate than the effects on achievement, there is reason to expect motivational effects to improve learning over time by mediating the relationship between altered practices and student achievement. Hence, we propose that mediated effects should also be tested over time (for example, across the two to three years following initial implementation). Identification and testing of such models would enhance our understanding of how and why interdisciplinary curriculum might affect achievement.

Looping has even less evidence attesting to its promise than the other three practices do. And the studies that point to the potential of looping (see Chapter Three) failed to control for many important student, school, and district characteristics, rendering it difficult to ascertain how looping affects student outcomes. More quantitative research needs to be undertaken to confirm the potential promise of looping.

Effects of Teacher Education

As Chapter Seven points out, investigating the effects of different training and professional development programs on student outcomes could be a powerful way to improve teacher education for middle grades. There should be efforts to study the effects of training (such as learning about classroom management or instructional methods) on classroom practices and also how these practices in turn affect student outcomes (for example, disciplinary problems or achievement). There may not be strong direct associations between new types of training on student behavior and performance, but changes in classroom practices may account for such effects. Thus, this type of research applies the test of mediation for evaluation purposes. If gains in student achievement (or decreased disciplinary problems) could be demonstrated as a function of training using such models, middle school advocates would be better prepared to argue for changes in current teacher preparation or professional development programs.

In addition, researchers should continue to test and compare various models of teacher preparation. In light of the current policy debates regarding a middle school certification, it would be particularly relevant to test how middle school–specific training compares with typical secondary school training combined with subsequent professional development on adolescent development and additional field experience influence student outcomes.

Effects of Parental Involvement

Most of the research on this topic is correlational; hence, it is not clear whether increased parental involvement improves children's academic success or whether parents of high-achieving children are more involved (see Chapter Eight). Of course, it would be unethical to conduct an experiment that randomly assigned students to conditions of "low-quality parental involvement" and "high-quality parental involvement," but there is certainly room for further empirical research.

One possible design for future research would be a multiple-baseline experiment, which would provide an intervention (for example, increased efforts on the part of the schools to provide information and advice to parents) to multiple groups but to each group at a different time. Using time as the control can then reveal whether the intervention effected the changes in the outcomes (such as student achievement). Bringing this method to the study of parental involvement would allow researchers to take a proactive approach and conduct interventions on classrooms or entire schools at different times. There would undoubtedly be many factors to control for (for example, possible barriers to involvement, such as parents' working hours and levels of education), but such a study would show (a) whether parental involvement can be increased (and sustained) and (b) whether increased involvement indeed boosts the school performance and adaptive functioning of young teens.

References

Adelman, H. S., L. Taylor, and M. V Schnieder, "A School-Wide Component to Address Barriers to Learning," *Reading and Writing Quarterly*, Vol. 15, No. 4, 1999, pp. 277–302.

Alexander, W., "The Middle School Emerges and Flourishes," in J. Lounsbury, ed., *Perspectives: Middle School Education, 1964–1984,* Columbus, Ohio: National Middle Schools Association, 1984, p. 15.

Alexander, K. L., and D. R. Entwisle, "School and Children at Risk," in Booth and Dunn (1996), pp. 67–88.

Alexander, K. L., D. R. Entwisle, and N. Kabbani, "The Dropout Process in Life Course Perspective: Early Risk Factors at Home and School," *Teachers College Record,* Vol. 103, No. 5, 2001, pp. 760–822.

Alexander, W. M., and P. S. George, *The Exemplary Middle School*, New York: CBS College Publishing, 1981.

Alexander, W. M., and C. K. McEwin, *Schools in the Middle: Status and Progress*, Columbus, Ohio: National Middle School Association, 1989.

Alspaugh, J. W., "Achievement Loss Associated with the Transition to Middle School and High School," *The Journal of Educational Research*, September/October 1998, Vol. 92, No. 1, p. 20.

Alspaugh, J. W., and R. D. Harting, "Transition Effects of School Grade-Level Organization on Student Achievement," *Journal of Research and Development in Education*, Vol. 28, No. 3, 1995, pp. 145–149.

Alt, M. N., and S. P. Choy, *In the Middle: Characteristics of Public Schools with a Focus on Middle Schools*, Washington, D.C.: U.S. Government Printing Office, NCES 2000-312, 2000.

Anafra, V. A., ed., *The Handbook of Research in Middle Level Education*, Greenwich, Conn.: Information Age Publishing, 2001.

Anafra, V.A., and K. M. Brown, "Advisor-Advisee Programs: Community Building in a State of Affective Disorder?" in Anafra (2001), pp. 3–34.

Anderman, E. M., and M. L. Maehr, "Motivation and Schooling in the Middle Grades," *Review of Educational Research*, Vol. 64, No. 2, 1994, pp. 287–309.

Arhar, J. M., "Interdisciplinary Teaming and the Social Bonding of Middle Level Students," in J. L. Irvin, ed., *Transforming Middle Level Education: Perspectives and Possibilities*, Boston: Allyn and Bacon, 1992, pp. 139–161.

_____, "The Effects of Interdisciplinary Teaming on Teachers and Students," in Irvin (1997), pp. 49–55.

Atanda, R., "Do Gatekeeper Courses Expand Education Options?" *Education Statistics Quarterly*, Vol. 1, No. 1, Spring 1999. Also available online at http://nces.ed.gov/pubs99/quarterly/spring/4-elementary/4-esq11-c.html (as of October 17, 2003).

Aunola, K., H. Stattin, and J. E. Nurmi, "Adolescents' Achievement Strategies, School Adjustment, and Externalizing and Internalizing Problem Behaviors," *Journal of Youth and Adolescence*, Vol. 29, 2000, pp. 289–306.

Balfanz, R., D. J. MacIver, and D. Ryan, "Achieving Algebra for All with a Facilitated Instructional Program: First Year Results of the Talent Development Middle School Mathematics Program," paper presented at the annual meeting of the American Educational Research Association, Montreal, April 19–23, 1999.

Battistich, V., D. Solomon, D. Kim, M. Watson, and E. Schaps, "Schools as Communities, Poverty Levels of Student Populations, and Students' Attitudes, Motives, and Performance: A Multilevel Analysis," *American Educational Research Journal*, Vol. 32, 1995, pp. 627–658.

Battistich, V., D. Solomon, M. Watson, and E. Schaps, "Caring School Communities," *Educational Psychologist*, Vol. 32, No. 3, 1997, pp. 137–151.

Beane, J. A., *A Middle School Curriculum: From Rhetoric to Reality*, 2nd ed., Columbus, Ohio: National Middle School Association, 1993.

_____, " Introduction: What Is a Coherent Curriculum?" in J. Beane, ed., *Toward a Coherent Curriculum*, Alexandria, Va.: Association for Supervision and Curriculum Development, 1995, pp. 1–54.

_____, "Introduction: Reform and Reinvention," in T. S. Dickinson, ed., *Reinventing the Middle School*, New York: RoutledgeFalmer, 2001, pp. xiii–xxii.

Becker, B. E., and S. S. Luthar, "Social-Emotional Factors Affecting Achievement Outcomes Among Disadvantaged Students: Closing the Achievement Gap," *Educational Psychologist*, No. 37, 2002, pp. 197–214.

Bedard, K., "Are Middle Schools More Effective? The Impact of School System Configuration on Student Outcomes," unpublished paper currently under review, Santa Barbara, Calif.: Department of Economics, University of California, 2003.

Berends, M., S. J. Bodilly, and S. Kirby, *Facing the Challenges of Whole-School Reform: New American Schools After a Decade*, Santa Monica, Calif.: RAND Corporation, MR-1498-EDU, 2002.

Berman, P., and M. McLaughlin, "Implementation of Educational Innovations," *Educational Forum*, Vol. 40, 1978, pp. 347–370.

Black, S. "Together Again," *The American School Board Journal*, Vol. 187, No. 6, 2000, pp. 40–43.

Booth, A., and J. F. Dunn, eds., *Family-School Links: How Do They Affect Educational Outcomes?* Mahwah, N.J.: Lawrence Erlbaum Associates, 1996.

Bossing, N., and R. Cramer, *The Junior High School*, Boston: Houghton Mifflin Co., 1965.

Bottoms, G., S. Cooney, and K. Carpenter, *Improving the Middle Grades: Actions that Can Be Taken Now*, Atlanta, Ga.: Southern Regional Education Board, February 2003. Online at http://www.sreb.org.

Braddock, J. H., "Tracking the Middle Grades: National Patterns of Grouping for Instruction," *Phi Delta Kappan*, Vol. 71, 1990, pp. 445–449.

Bradley, A., and K. K. Manzo, "The Weak Link," *Education Week*, October 4, 2000.

Brand, Stephen, R. Felner, M. Shim, A. Seitsinger, and T. Dumas, "Middle School Improvement and Reform: Development and Validation of a School-Level Assessment of Climate, Cultural Pluralism, and School Safety," *Journal of Educational Psychology*, Vol. 95, No. 3, September 2003, pp. 570–588.

Braswell, J. S., A. D. Lutkus, W. S. Grigg, S. L. Santapau, B. Tay-Lim, and M. Johnson, *The Nation's Report Card: Mathematics 2000*, Washington, D.C.: U.S. Government Printing Office, NCES 2001-028, 2001.

Brewer, D. J., "Principal and Student Outcomes: Evidence from U.S. High Schools," *Economics of Education Review*, No. 12, 1993, pp. 281–292.

Brough, J. A., "Middle Level Education: An Historical Perspective," in M. Wavering, ed., *Educating Young Adolescents: Life in the Middle*, New York: Garland Publishing, 1995, pp. 27–51.

Brown, C., *Opportunities and Accountability to Leave No Child Behind in the Middle Grades: An Examination of the No Child Left Behind Act of 2001*, New York: Edna McConnell Clark Foundation, March 2002.

Brown, K. M., "Get the Big Picture of Teaming: Eliminate Isolation and Competition Through Focus, Leadership, and Professional Development," in Anafra (2001), pp. 35–72.

Cairns, B. D., and R. D. Cairns, *Lifelines and Risks: Pathways of Youth in Our Time*, New York: Cambridge University Press, 1994.

Campbell, J. R., C. M. Hombo, and J. Mazzeo, *NAEP 1999 Trends in Academic Progress: Three Decades of Student Performance*, Washington, D.C.: U.S. Government Printing Office, NCES 2000-469, 2000.

Carnegie—*See* Carnegie Council on Adolescent Development.

Carnegie Council on Adolescent Development, *Turning Points: Preparing American Youth for the 21st Century*, New York: Carnegie Corporation of New York, 1989.

Carnevale, A. P., *Education = Success: Empowering Hispanic Youths and Adults*, Princeton, N.J.: Educational Testing Service, 1999.

Carolina Population Center, National Longitudinal Study of Adolescent Health: Wave I Adolescent In-Home Questionnaire, electronic data file, Atlanta, Ga.: Public Health Service, Centers for Disease Control and Prevention, 1997.

Carroll, D., *National Education Longitudinal Study of 1988 Eighth Graders, Third Follow-Up*, Washington, D.C.: U.S. Government Printing Office, NCES 2000-328, 2000.

Carter, R. S., and R. A. Wojtkiewicz, "Parental Involvement with Adolescents' Education: Do Daughters or Sons Get More Help?" *Adolescence*, Vol. 35, No. 137, 2000, pp. 29–44.

Cattcrall, J. S., *Different Ways of Knowing 1991–1994 Longitudinal Study Final Report: Program Effects on Students and Teachers*, Los Angeles: University of California, 1995.

Center for Research on Elementary and Middle Schools, John Hopkins University, "Implementation and Effects of the Middle Grades Practices," CREMS Report, March 1990, 6.

Center on School, Family, and Community Partnerships at Johns Hopkins University, Web site, no date. Online at http://www.csos.jhu.edu/p2000/center.htm (as of October 23, 2003).

Chandler, K. A., M. J. Nolin, and E. Davies, *Student Strategies to Avoid Harm at School*, Washington, D.C.: U.S. Government Printing Office, NCES 95-203, 1995.

Chaney, B., *Student Outcomes and the Professional Preparation of Eighth-Grade Teachers in Science and Mathematics*, Rockville, Md.: Westat, Inc., May 1995.

Chen, X., *Efforts by Public K–8 Schools to Involve Parents in Children's Education: Do School and Parent Reports Agree?* Washington, D.C.: U.S. Government Printing Office, NCES 2001–076, 2001.

Chubb, J. E., and T. M. Moe, *What Price Democracy? Politics, Markets, and America's Schools*, Washington, D.C.: Brookings Institution, 1990.

Cobb, B. R., S. Abate, and D. Baker, "Effects on Students of a 4 x 4 Junior High School Block Scheduling Program," *Educational Policy Analysis Archives*, Vol. 7, No. 3, February 8, 1999. Online at http://epaa.asu.edu/epaa/v7n3.html (as of October 21, 2003).

Cohen, J., *Statistical Power Analysis for the Behavioral Sciences*, 2nd ed., Hillsdale, N.J.: Lawrence Erlbaum Associates, 1988.

Cole, D., "Relation of Social and Academic Competence to Depressive Symptoms in Childhood," *Journal of Abnormal Psychology*, No. 99, 1990, pp. 422–429.

Cook, T. D. "Inequality in Educational Achievement: Families Are the Source, but Are Schools Prophylactic?" in Booth and Dunn (1996), pp. 89–106.

Cook, T. D., F. Habib, M. Philips, R. Settersten, S. C. Shagle, and S. M. Degirmencioglu, "Comer's School Development Program in Prince George's County, Maryland: A Theory-Based Evaluation," *American Educational Research Journal*, Vol. 36, No. 3, 1999, pp. 543–597.

Cooney, S., "Education's Weak Link: Student Performance in the Middle Grades," paper, Atlanta, Ga.: Southern Regional Education Board, March 1998a. Online at http://

www.sreb.org/programs/MiddleGrades/publications/reports/weaklink.pdf (as of October 21, 2003).

_____, "Improving Teaching in the Middle Grades: Higher Standards for Students Aren't Enough," paper, Atlanta, Ga.: Southern Regional Education Board, December 1998b.

Cooney, S., and G. Bottoms, "A Highly Qualified Teacher in Every Middle Grades Classroom: What States, Districts, and Schools Can Do," paper, Atlanta, Ga.: Southern Regional Education Board, February 2003.

Cooper H., B. Nye, K. Charlton, J. J. Lindsey, and S. Greathouse, "The Effects of Summer Vacation on Achievement Test Scores: A Narrative and Analytic Review," *Review of Educational Research*, Vol. 66, 1996, pp. 227–268.

Cooper, H., J. C. Valentine, K. Charlton, and A. Melson, "The Effects of Modified School Calendars on Student Achievement and on School and Community Attitudes," *Review of Educational Research*, Vol. 73, 2003, pp. 1–52.

Cuban, L., "What Happens to Reforms That Last? The Case of the Junior High School," *American Educational Research Journal*, Vol. 29, 1992, pp. 227–251.

Darling-Hammond, L., "Teacher Quality and Student Achievement: A Review of State Policy Evidence," *Education Policy Analysis Archives*, Vol. 8, No. 1, January 1, 2000. Online at http://epaa.asu.edu/epaa/v8n1/ (as of October 21, 2003).

Dauber, S. L., and J. L. Epstein, *Parent Attitudes and Practices of Parent Involvement in Inner-City Elementary and Middle Schools*, Baltimore: The John Hopkins University Center for Social Organization of Schools, CREMS Report 33, 1989.

DePascale, C. A., *Education Reform Restructuring Network: Impact Documentation Report*, Cambridge, Mass.: Data Analysis & Testing Associates, 1997.

Desimone, L. M., A. C. Porter, M. S. Garet, K. S. Yoon, and B. F. Birman, "Effects of Professional Development on Teachers' Instruction: Results from a Three-Year Longitudinal Study," *Educational Evaluation and Policy Analysis*, Vol. 24, No. 2, 2002, pp. 81–112.

Dickinson, T. S., "Reinventing the Middle School: A Proposal to Counter Arrested Development," in T. S. Dickinson, ed., *Reinventing the Middle School*, New York: RoutledgeFalmer, 2001, pp. 1–20.

Dishion, T. J., J. McCord, and F. Poulin, "When Interventions Harm: Peer Groups and Problem Behavior," *American Psychologist*, Vol. 54, 1999, pp. 755–764.

Donahue, P. L., K. E. Voelkl, J. R. Campbell, and J. Mazzeo, *1998 Reading Report Card for the Nation and the States*, Washington, D.C.: U.S. Government Printing Office, NCES 1999-500, 1999.

Dornbusch, S. M., and K. L. Glasgow, "The Structural Context of Family-School Relations," in Booth and Dunn (1996), pp. 35–44.

Dryfoos, J. G., Adolescents at Risk: Prevalence and Prevention, New York: Oxford University Press, 1990.

_____, "Full Service Schools: Revolution or Fad?" *Journal of Research on Adolescence*, Vol. 5, No. 2, 1995, pp. 147–172.

Eccles, J. S., and R. D. Harold, Family Involvement in Children's and Adolescents' Schooling. " in Booth and Dunn (1996), pp. 3–34.

Eccles, J. S., and C. Midgley, "Stage/Environment Fit: Developmentally Appropriate Classrooms for Early Adolescents," in R. Ames and C. Ames, eds., *Research on Motivation in Education*, Vol. 3, San Diego, Calif.: Academic, 1989, pp. 139–186.

Eccles, J. S., S. Lord, and C. Midgley, "What Are We Doing to Adolescents? The Impact of Educational Contexts on Early Adolescents," *American Journal of Education*, Vol. 99, 1991, pp. 52–542.

Eccles, J. S., C. Midgley, A. Wigfield, C. M. Buchanan, D. Reuman, C. Flanagan, and D. MacIver, "Development During Adolescence: The Impact of Stage-Environment Fit On Adolescents' Experiences in Schools and Families," *American Psychologist*, No. 48, 1993, pp. 90–101.

"To Close the Gap, Quality Counts," *Education Week, Quality Counts 2003*, Vol. 22, No. 17, 2003, pp. 7.

Educational Testing Service, *Dreams Deferred: High School Dropouts in the United States*, Princeton, N.J., 1995.

Ekstrom, R. B., M. E. Goertz, J. M. Pollack, and D. A. Rock, "Who Drops Out of High School and Why? Findings from a National Study," Educational Testing Service, No. 87, 1986, pp. 356–373.

Eliot, C. W., *Educational Reform: Essays and Addresses*, New York: The Century Co., 1898.

Elmore, R. F., "Bridging the Gap Between Standards and Achievement: The Imperative for Professional Development in Education," Washington, D.C.: The Albert Shanker Institute, 2002. Online at http://www.shankerinstitute.org/Downloads/Bridging_Gap.pdf (as of October 21, 2003).

Epstein, J. L., and S. Lee, "National Patterns of School and Family Connections in the Middle Grades," in Ryan et al. (1995), pp. 108–154.

Epstein, J. L., B. S. Simon, and K. C. Salinas, "Involving Parent in Homework in the Middle Grades," 1997. Online at http://www.pdkintl.org/edres/resbul18.htm (as of October 21, 2003).

Falbo, T., L. Lein, and N. A. Amador, "Parental Involvement During the Transition to High School," *Journal of Adolescent Research*, No. 16, 2001, pp. 511–529.

Farkas, S., J. Johnson, A. Duffett, T. Foleno, and P. Foley, *Trying to Stay Ahead of the Game: Superintendents and Principals Talk about Schools Leadership*, New York: Public Agenda, 2001.

Felner, R. D., S. Brand, A. M. Adan, P. F. Mulhall, N. Flowers, B. Sartain, and D. L. DuBois, "Restructuring the Ecology of the School as an Approach to Prevention During School Transitions: Longitudinal Follow-Ups and Extensions of the School

Transitional Environment Project (STEP)," *Prevention in Human Services*, Vol. 10, No. 2, 1993, pp. 103–136.

Felner, R. D., S. Brand, D. L. DuBois, A. Adan, et al., "Socioeconomic Disadvantage, Proximal Environmental Experiences, and Socioemotional and Academic Adjustment in Early Adolescence: Investigation of a Mediated Effects Model," *Child Development*, No. 66, 1995, pp. 774–792.

Felner, R. D., A. W. Jackson, D. Kasak, P. Mulhall, S. Brand, and N. Flowers, "The Impact of School Reform for the Middle Years: Longitudinal Study of a Network Engaged in Turning Points-Based Comprehensive School Transformation," *Phi Delta Kappan*, Vol. 78, No. 7, 1997, pp. 528–550.

Finn, J. D., "Withdrawing from School," *Review of Educational Research*, No. 59, 1989, pp. 117–142.

_____, *School Engagement and Students at Risk,* Washington, D.C.: Government Printing Office, NCES 1993–470, 1993.

Finn, J. D., and C. M. Achilles, "Tennessee's Class Size Study: Findings, Implications, Misconceptions," *Educational Evaluation and Policy Analysis*, Vol. 21, 1999, pp. 97–109.

Fiore, T. A., and T. R. Curtin, *Public and Private School Principals in the United States: A Statistical Profile, 1987–88 to 1993–94*, Washington, D.C.: U.S. Department of Education, National Center for Education Statistics, 1997.

Flowers, N., S. B. Mertens, and P. F. Mulhall, "The Impact of Teaming: Five Research-Based Outcomes of Teaming," *Middle School Journal*, Vol. 31, No. 2, 1999, pp. 57–60.

_____, "What Makes Interdisciplinary Teams Effective?" *Middle School Journal,* Vol. 31, No. 3, 2000, pp. 53–56.

_____, "Four Important Lessons About Teacher Professional Development," *Middle School Journal*, May 2002, p. 57.

Foy, P., "Implementation of the TIMSS Sample Design," in M. O. Martin and D. L. Kelly, eds., *TIMSS Technical Manual*, Vol. II: *Implementation and Analysis Primary and Middle School Years*, Chestnut Hill, Mass.: Boston College, 1998, pp. 21–45.

Galassi, J. P., S. A. Gulledge, and N. A. Cox, "Middle School Advisories: Retrospect and Prospect," *Review of Educational Research*, Vol. 67, No. 3, 1997, pp. 301–338.

Gaskill, P. E., "Progress in the Certification of Middle-Level Personnel," *Middle School Journal*, Vol. 33, No. 5, 2002, pp. 33–40.

Gentry, M., R. K. Gable, and M. G. Rizza, "Students Perceptions of Classroom Activities: Are There Grade-Level and Gender Differences?" *Journal of Educational Psychology*, Vol. 94, No. 3, 2002, pp. 539–544.

George, P., *No Child Left Behind: Implications for Middle Level Leaders*, Westerville, Ohio: National Middle School Association, 2003.

George, P. S., "A Middle School—If You Can Keep It; Part II," Midpoints: Occasional Papers, Westerville, Ohio: National Middle School Association, 1999.

George, P. S., and W. M. Alexander, *The Exemplary Middle School*, 2nd ed., New York: Holt, Reinhart, and Winston, Inc., 1993.

Goh, S. C., "Psychosocial Climate and Student Outcomes in Elementary Mathematics Classrooms: A Multilevel Analysis," *Journal of Experimental Education*, No. 64, 1995, pp. 29–40.

Gonazalez, P., C. Calsyn, L. Jocelyn, K. Mak, D. Kastberg, S. Arafeh, T. Williams, and W. Tsen, *Pursuing Excellence: Comparisons of International Eighth-Grade Mathematics and Science Achievement from a U.S. Perspective, 1995 and 1999*, Washington, D.C.: U.S. Government Printing Office, NCES 2001-028, December 2000. Online at http://nces.ed.gov/pubsearch/pubsinfo.asp?pubid=2001028 (as of December 4, 2003).

Goodenow, C., "Classroom Belonging Among Early Adolescent Students: Relationships to Motivation and Achievement," *Journal of Early Adolescence*, Vol. 13, 1993, pp. 21–43.

Gottfredson, G. D., D. C. Gottfredson, E. R. Czeh, D. Cantor, S. B. Crosse, and I. Hantman, *National Study of Delinquency Prevention in Schools*, final report, Elliot City, Md.: Gottfredson Associates, Inc., 2000.

Grant, J., "In the Loop," *School Administrator*, Vol. 57, No. 1, 2000, pp. 30–33.

Grant, T. M., "The Legal and Psychological Implications of Tracking in Education," *Law and Psychology Review*, No. 15, 1991, pp. 299–312.

Gross, S., "Early Mathematics Performance and Achievement: Results of a Study Within a Large Suburban School System," *Journal of Negro Education*, Vol. 62, No. 3, 1993, pp. 269–285.

Gruhn, W., and H. Douglass, *The Modern Junior High School*, 2nd ed., New York: Ronald Press, 1956.

Hall, S. G., *Adolescence: Its Psychology and Its Relations to Physiology, Anthropology, Sociology, Sex, Crime, Religion and Education*, Vol. II, New York: D. Appleton & Co, 1905.

Hallinger, P., and R. Heck, "Reassessing the Principal's Role in School Effectiveness: A Review of Empirical Research, 1980–95," *Education Administration Quarterly*, No. 32, 1996, pp. 5–44.

Haskins, R., T. Walden, and C. T. Ramey, "Teacher and Student Behavior in High- and Low-Ability Groups," *Journal of Educational Psychology*, No. 75, 1983, pp. 865–867.

Hawk, P., C. R. Coble, and M. Swanson, "Certification: It Does Matter," *Journal of Teacher Education*, Vol. 36, No. 3, 1985, pp. 13–15.

Haycock, K., and N. Ames, "Where Are We Now? Taking Stock of Middle Grades Education," keynote address at the National Educational Research Policy and Priorities Board's Conference on Curriculum, Instruction, and Assessment in the Middle Grades: Linking Research and Practice, Washington, D.C., July 24–25, 2000.

Heaviside, S., C. Rowand, C. Williams, E. Farris, S. Burns, and E. McArthur, *Violence and Discipline Problems in Public Schools: 1996–97*, Washington, D.C.: U.S. Government Printing Office, NCES 98030, 1998.

Henderson, A. T., and K. L. Mapp, *A New Wave of Evidence the Impact of School, Family, and Community Connections on Student Achievement*, Austin, Tex.: Southwest Educational Development Laboratory, National Center for Family and Community Connections with Schools, 2002.

Ho Sui-Chu, E., and J. D. Willms, "Effects of Parental Involvement on Eighth-Grade Achievement," *Sociology of Education*, Vol. 69, 1996, pp. 126–141.

Hoagwood, K., "Issues in Designing and Implementing Studies of Non-Mental Health Care Sectors," *Journal of Clinical Child Psychology*, No. 23, 1995, pp. 114–120.

Hough, D., "The Elemiddle School: A Model for Middle Grades Reform," *Principal*, Vol. 74, No. 3, 1995, pp. 6–9.

_____, *R3 = Research, Rhetoric, and Reality: A Study of Studies*, Westerville, Ohio National Middle School Association, 2003.

Howe, A. C., and J. Bell, "Factors Associated With Successful Implementation of Interdisciplinary Curriculum Units," *Research in Middle Level Education Quarterly*, Vol. 21, No. 2, 1998, pp. 39–52.

Hutcheson, J., and T. E. Moeller, "Using Evaluation to Recreate a Middle Level Teacher Education Program," *Middle School Journal*, Vol. 26, No. 5, 1995, pp. 32–36.

Ingels, S. J., K. Dowd, J. Baldridge, J. L. Stipe, J. H. Bartot, and M. R. Frankel, *NELS:88 Second Follow-Up: Student Component Data User's Manual*, Washington, D.C.: U.S. Government Printing Office, NCES 94-374, October 1994. Also online at http://nces.ed.gov/pubsearch/pubsinfo.asp?pubid=94374 (as of October 17, 2003).

Ingersoll, R. M., "The Problem of Underqualified Teachers in American Secondary Schools," *Educational Researcher*, Vol. 28, No. 2, March 1999, pp. 26–37.

Irvin, J., ed., *What Current Research Says to the Middle Level Practitioner*, Columbus, Ohio: National Middle School Association, 1997.

Jackson, A. W., and G. A. Davis, *Turning Points 2000: Educating Adolescents in the 21st Century*, New York: Teachers College Press, 2000.

Jessor, R., and S. Jessor, *Problem Behavior and Psychosocial Development: A Longitudinal Study of Youth*, New York: Academic Press, 1977.

"Joel Klein's First Day of School," *The New York Times*, editorial, September 5, 2002, p. A-22.

Juvonen, J., "School Violence: Prevalence, Precursors, and Prevention," *ERS Spectrum*, Vol. 20, 2002, pp. 4–10.

Juvonen, J., and S. Graham, eds., *Peer Harassment in School: The Plight of the Vulnerable and Victimized*, New York: Guilford Press, 2001.

Juvonen, J., and S. Graham, "Research Based Interventions on Bullying," in C. E. Sanders and G. D. Phye, eds., *Bullying, Implications for the Classroom: What Does the Research Say?* New York: Academic Press, in press.

Juvonen, J., A. Nishina, and S. Graham, "Self-Views and Peer Perceptions of Victim Status Among Early Adolescents," in Juvonen and Graham (2001), pp. 105–124.

Kaplan, D. S., B. M. Peck, and H. B. Kaplan, "Decomposing the Academic Failure–Dropout Relationship: A Longitudinal Analysis," *Journal of Educational Research*, No. 90, 1997, pp. 331–343.

Kauchak, D. P., and P. D. Eggen, *Learning and Teaching: Research-Based Methods*, 3rd ed., Needham Heights, Mass.: Allyn and Bacon, 1998.

Kazdin, A. E., "Adolescent Mental Health: Prevention and Treatment Programs," *American Psychologist*, No. 48, 1993, pp. 127–141.

Keating, D. P., "Adolescent Thinking," in S. Feldman and G. Elliot, eds., *At the Threshold: The Developing Adolescent*, Cambridge, Mass.: Harvard University Press, 1990, pp. 54–89.

Keith, T. Z., and P. Keith, "Does Parental Involvement Affect Eighth-Grade Student Achievement? Structural Analysis of National Data," *School Psychology Review*, Vol. 22, No. 3, 1993, pp. 474–496.

Kellam, S., G. Ling, R. Merisca, C. H. Brown, and N. Ialongo, "The Effect of the Level of Aggression in the First Grade Classroom on the Course and Malleability of Aggressive Behavior into Middle School," *Development and Psychopathology*, No. 10, 1998, pp. 165–185.

Kershaw, T., "The Effects of Educational Tracking on the Social Mobility of African Americans," *Journal of Black Studies*, No. 23, 1992, pp. 125–169.

Kessler, R. C., C. L. Foster, W. B. Saunders, and P. E. Stang, "Social Consequences of Psychiatric Disorders, I: Educational Attainment," *American Journal of Psychiatry*, Vol. 152, No. 7, July 1995, pp. 1,026–1,032.

Killion, J., "What Works in the Middle: Results-Based Staff Development," New York: Edna McConnell Clark Foundation, 1999.

King, M. B., "Professional Development to Promote School-Wide Inquiry," *Teaching and Teacher Education*, Vol. 18, 2002, pp. 243–257.

Kingery, P. M., M. B. Coggeshall, and A. A. Alford, "Violence at School: Recent Evidence from Four National Surveys," *Psychology in the Schools*, No. 35, 1998, pp. 247–258.

Kirby, S. N., M. Berends, and S. Naftel, *Implementation in a Longitudinal Sample of New American Schools: Four Years into Scale-Up*, Santa Monica, Calif.: RAND Corporation, MR-1413-EDU, 2001.

Knight, P., "A Systematic Approach to Professional Development: Learning as Practice," *Teaching and Teacher Education*, Vol. 18, 2002, pp. 229–241.

Kuperminc, G., B. Leadbeater, and S. Blatt, "School Social Climate and Individual Differences in Vulnerability to Psychopathology Among Middle School Students," *Journal of School Psychology*, Vol. 39, No. 2, 2001, pp. 141–159.

Lee, V. E., and D. T. Burkam, "Inequality at the Starting Gate: Social Background Differences in Achievement as Children Begin School," Washington, D.C.: Economic Policy

Institute, 2002. Online at http://www.epinet.org/content.cfm/books_starting_gate (as of October 21, 2003).

Lee, V. E., and J. B. Smith, "Effects of School Restructuring on the Achievement and Engagement of Middle-Grade Students," *Sociology of Education*, Vol. 66, No. 3, 1993, pp. 164–187.

_____, "Social Support and Achievement for Young Adolescents in Chicago: The Role of School Academic Press," *American Educational Research Journal*, Vol. 36, 1999, pp. 907–945.

Lee, V. E., J. B. Smith, T. E. Perry, and M. A. Smylie, "Social Support, Academic Press, and Student Achievement: A View from the Middle Grades in Chicago," Chicago: Consortium on Chicago School Research, October 1999.

Lieberman, A., "Practices That Support Teacher Development," *Phi Delta Kappan*, Vol. 76, 1995, pp. 591–596.

Lieberman, A., and D. Wood, "When Teachers Write: Of Networks and Learning," in A. Lieberman and L. Miller, eds., *Teachers Caught in the Action: Professional Development that Matters*, New York: Teachers College Press, 2001.

Lincoln, R. D., "Looping in the Middle Grades," *Principal*, Vol. 78, No. 1, 1998, pp. 58–59.

Linn, R. L., E. L. Baker, and D. W. Betebenner, "Accountability Systems: Implications of Requirements of the No Child Left Behind Act of 2001," *Educational Researcher*, Vol. 31, No. 6, 2002, pp. 3–16.

Lipsey, M. W., "The Effect of Treatment on Juvenile Delinquents: Results from Meta-Analysis," in F. Loesel and D. Bender, eds., *Psychology and Law: International Perspectives*, Berlin: Walter De Gruyter, 1992, pp. 131–143.

Lipsitz, J., *Growing Up Forgotten: A Review of Research and Programs Concerning Early Adolescence*, New Brunswick, N.J.: Transaction Books, 1980.

Lipsitz, J., A. W. Jackson, and L. M. Austin, "What Works in Middle-Grades School Reform," *Phi Delta Kappan*, Vol. 78, No. 7, 1997, pp. 517.

Lipsitz, J., M. H. Mizell, A. W. Jackson, and L. M. Austin, "Speaking With One Voice: A Manifesto for Middle-Grade Reform," *Phi Delta Kappan*, Vol. 78, No. 7, March 1997, pp. 533–540.

Lord, S., J. S. Eccles, and K. McCarthy, "Risk and Protective Factors in Transition to Junior High School," *Journal of Early Adolescence*, No. 14, 1994, pp. 162–199.

Lounsbury, J., and J. H. Johnston, *Life in the Three Sixth Grade*, Reston, Va.: National Association of Secondary School Principals, 1988.

MacIver, D. J., and J. L. Epstein, "Responsive Practices in the Middle Grades: Teacher Teams, Advisory Groups, Remedial Instruction, and School Transition Programs," *American Journal of Education*, Vol. 99, 1991, pp. 587–622.

MacIver, D. J., S. B. Plank, and R. Balfanz, *Working Together to Become Proficient Readers: Early Impact of the Talent Development Middle School's Student Team Literature Program*, Baltimore, Md.: Center for Research on the Education of Students Placed at Risk, 1997.

MacIver, D. J., A. Ruby, R. Balfanz, and V. Byrnes, "Removed from the List: A Comparative Longitudinal Case Study of a Reconstitution-Eligible School," *Journal of Curriculum and Supervision*, Vol. 18, No. 3, 2003, pp. 259–289.

Mackinnon, A., *Standards-Based Middle Grades Reform in Six Urban Districts, 1995–2001*, New York: Edna McConnell Clark Foundation, 2003. Online at http://www.emcf.org/programs/student/student_pub.htm (as of October 21, 2003).

Masten, A. S., and J. D. Coatsworth, "The Development of Competence in Favorable and Unfavorable Environments," *American Psychologist*, No. 53, 1998, pp. 205–220.

McEwin, C. K., and T. S. Dickinson, "Essential Elements in the Preparation of Middle Level Teachers," in Irvin (1997), pp. 223–229.

McEwin, C. K., T. S. Dickinson, and D. M. Jenkins, *America's Middle Schools: Practices and Progress: A 25-Year Perspective*, Columbus, Ohio: National Middle School Association, 1996.

McEwin, C. K., T. S. Dickinson, and J. Swaim, "Middle Level Teacher Preparation: A National Status Report," working paper, Boone, N.C.: Appalachian State University, 1996.

McMahon, T. J., N. L. Ward, M. K. Pruett, L. Davidson, and E. H. Griffith, "Building Full-Service Schools: Lessons Learned in the Development of Interagency Collaboratives," *Journal of Educational & Psychological Consultation*, Vol. 11, No. 1, 2000, pp. 65–92.

McNeely, C. A., J. M. Nonnemaker, and R. Blum, "Promoting School Connectedness: Evidence from the National Longitudinal Study of Adolescent Health," *Journal of School Health*, Vol. 72, No. 4, 2002, pp. 138–146.

McPartland, J. M., "How Departmentalized Staffing and Interdisciplinary Teaming Combine for Effects on Middle Grade Students," paper presented at the annual meeting of the American Educational Research Association, Chicago, April 3–7, 1991.

Mertens, S. B., N. Flowers, and P. Mulhall, *The Middle Start Initiative, Phase I: A Longitudinal Analysis of Michigan Middle-Level Schools*, Urbana, Ill.: University of Illinois, Institute of Government and Public Affairs, Center for Prevention Research and Development, 1998. Online at http://www.cprd.uiuc.edu (as of October 21, 2003).

_____, "The Relationship Between Middle-Grades Teachers Certification and Teaching Practices," *Middle School Curriculum*, Instruction, and Assessment, 2002, pp. 119–138.

Midgley, C., and K. Edelin, "Middle School Reform and Early Adolescent Well-Being: The Good News and the Bad," *Educational Psychologist*, Vol. 33, No. 4, 1998, pp. 195–206.

Midgley, C., and H. Feldlaufer, "Students' and Teachers' Decision-Making Fit Before and After the Transition to Junior High School," *Journal of Early Adolescence*, Vol. 7, 1987, pp. 225–241.

Midgley, C., H. Feldlaufer, and J. Eccles, "The Transition to Junior High School: Beliefs of Pre- and Posttransition Teachers," *Journal of Youth and Adolescence*, Vol. 17, No. 6, 1988, pp. 543–562.

Mitman, A. L., A. L. Lash, and J. R. Mergendeller, "The Relationship of School Program Features to the Attitudes and Performance of Early Adolescents," *Journal of Early Adolescence*, Vol. 5, No. 2, 1985, pp. 161–182.

Mizell, M. H., Shooting for the Sun: the Message of Middle School Reform, selected remarks, New York: The Edna McDonnell Clark Foundation, 2002.

Monk, D. H., "Subject Area Preparation of Secondary Mathematics and Science Teachers and Student Achievement," *Economics of Education Review*, Vol. 13, No. 2, 1994, pp. 125–145.

Monk, D. H., and J. K. King, "Multilevel Teacher Resource Effects on Pupil Performance in Secondary Mathematics and Science: The Case of Teacher Subject-Matter Preparation," in R. Ehrenberg, ed., *Choices and Consequences: Contemporary Policy Issues in Education*, Ithaca, N.Y.: ILR Press, 1994, pp. 29–58.

Mrazek, Patricia J., and Robert J. Haggerty, eds., *Reducing Risks for Mental Disorders: Frontiers for Preventive Intervention Research*, Washington, D.C.: National Academy Press, 1994.

Mulhall, P. F., S. B. Mertens, and N. Flowers, "How Familiar Are Parents with Middle Level Practices?" *Middle School Journal*, November 2001, pp. 57–61.

Mullis, I. V. S., M. O. Martin, A. E. Beaton, E. J. Gonzalez, D. L. Kelly, and T. A. Smith, *Mathematics and Science Achievement in the Final Year of Secondary School*, Chestnut Hill, Mass.: Boston College, 1998.

Mullis, I. V. S., M. O. Martin, E. J. Gonzalez, K. D. Gregory, T. A. Smith, S. J. Chrostowski, R. A. Garden, and K. M. O'Connor, *TIMSS 1999 International Mathematics Report: Findings from IEA's Repeat of the Third International Mathematics and Science Study at the 8th Grade*, Chestnut Hill, Mass.: Boston College, 2000.

Muth, K. and D. Alverman, *Teaching and Learning in the Middle Grades*, Needham Heights, Mass.: Allyn and Bacon, 1992.

Nansel, T. R., M. Overpeck, R. S. Pilla, W. J. Ruan, B. Simons-Morton, and P. Scheidt, "Bullying Behaviors Among U.S. Youth: Prevalence and Association with Psychosocial Adjustment," *Journal of the American Medical Association*, No. 285, 2001, pp. 2094–2100.

National Association for Elementary School Principals, Web site, 2003. Online at http://www.naesp.org/ (as of December 3, 2003).

National Center for Education Statistics, National Assessment of Educational Progress: The Nation's Report Card, Web site, 2003. Online at http://nces.ed.gov/nationsreportcard/ (as of October 29, 2003).

National Coalition for Parent Involvement in Education, Web site, 2003. Online at http://www.ncpie.org/ (as of October 23, 2003).

National Commission on Excellence in Education, *A Nation at Risk: The Imperative for Educational Reform*, Washington, D.C.: U.S. Department of Education, April 1983.

National Education Association, "Report of the Committee on College Entrance Requirements," *Journal of Proceedings and Addresses of the Thirty-Eighth Annual Meeting*, Los Angeles, 1899, pp. 632–817.

National Forum to Accelerate Middle School Reforms, Comprehensive School Reform Models, Web site, Newton, Mass., 2003. Online at http://www.mgforum.org/Improvingschools/CSR/csr_intro.htm (as of October 29, 2003).

National Institute on Educational Governance, Finance, Policymaking, and Management, *Effective Leaders for Today's Schools: Synthesis of a Policy Forum on Educational Leadership*, Washington, D.C.: U.S. Department of Education, Office of Educational Research and Improvement, 1999.

National Middle School Association, "This We Believe: Developmentally Responsive Middle Level Schools," position paper, Columbus, Ohio, 1995.

_____, "Parent Involvement and Student Achievement at the Middle Level," Research Summary No. 18, 2000. Online at http://www.nmsa.org/research/ressum18.htm (as of October 24, 2003).

National Parent Information Network, Web site, 2003. Online at http://npin.org (as of October 23, 2003).

National Parent Teacher Association, "National Standards for Parent/Family Involvement Programs," Web page, Chicago, Ill., 1998. Online at http://www.pta.org/programs/pfistand.htm (as of October 24, 2003).

_____, Web site, 2003. Online at http://www.pta.org/ (as of October 23, 2003).

National PTA—See National Parent Teacher Association.

National Research Council, Panel on High-Risk Youth, *Losing Generations: Adolescents in High Risk Settings*, Washington D.C.: National Academy Press, 1993.

Natriello, G., A. M. Pallas, and E. L. McDill, "A Population at Risk: Potential Consequences of Tougher School Standards for Student Dropouts," *American Journal of Education*, Vol. 94, 1986, pp. 135–181.

NMSA—See National Middle School Association.

Nolen-Hoksema, S., M. E. P. Seligman, and J. S. Girgus, "Predictors and Consequences of Childhood Depressive Symptoms: A 5-Year Longitudinal Study," *Journal of Abnormal Psychology*, No. 101, 1992, pp. 405–422.

North Central Regional Educational Laboratory, Changing by Design: Comprehensive School Reform, Web site, 1998. Online at http://www.ncrel.org (as of October 24, 2003).

Olweus, D., "Bully/Victim Problems Among School Children: Some Basic Facts and Effects of a School-Based Intervention Program," in D. Pepler and K. Rubin, eds., *The Development and Treatment of Childhood Aggression*, Hillsdale, N.J., 1991, pp. 411–448.

O'Sullivan, C. Y., M. A. Lauko, W. S. Grigg, J. Qian, and J. Zhang, *The Nation's Report Card: Science 2000*, NCES 2003-453, Washington, D.C.: U.S. Government Printing Office, 2003.

Pellegrino, J. W., L. R. Jones, and K. J. Mitchell, eds., *Grading the Nation's Report Card: Evaluating NAEP and Transforming The Assessment of Educational Progress*, Washington, D.C.: National Academy Press, 1999.

Perkins, D., *Smart Schools: From Training Memories to Educating Minds*, New York: The Free Press, 1992.

Peterson, J., M. Schwager, M. Crepeau, and K. Curry, *The Galef/WestEd Evaluation of San Francisco Unified School District's (SFUSD) Implementation of Different Ways of Knowing Report (DwoK)*, San Francisco: WestEd, 1998.

Petrosko, J. M., *Study A: Implementation of Student-Centered Teaching and Learning Practices and Student Assessment Results for Research Demonstration Site (RDS) Schools Participating in Different Ways of Knowing*, Louisville, Ky.: Galef Institute–Kentucky, Collaborative for Teaching and Learning, 1997.

Phillips, M., "What Makes Schools Effective? A Comparison of the Relationships of Communitarian Climate and Academic Climate to Mathematics Achievement and Attendance During Middle School," *American Educational Research Journal*, Vol. 34, No. 4, Winter 1997, pp. 633–662.

Pianta, R. C. and D. J. Walsh, *High-Risk Children in Schools: Constructing Sustaining Relationships*, New York: Routledge, 1996.

Price, H. B., "The Preparation Gap," *Education Week*, November 28, 2001.

Public Law 107–110, The No Child Left Behind Act of 2001, 115 Stat. 1425, January 8, 2002.

Putbrese, L., "Advisory Programs at the Middle Level: The Students' Response," *NASSP Bulletin*, No. 73, 1989, pp. 111–115.

Resnick, M. D., P. S. Bearman, R. W. Blum, K. E. Bauman, K. M. Harris, J. Jones, J. Tabor, T. Beuhring, R. E. Sieving, M. Shew, M. Ireland, L. H. Bearinger, and R. Udry, "Protecting Adolescents from Harm," *Journal of the American Medical Association*, Vol. 278, No. 10, 1997, pp. 823–832.

Rettig, M. D., and R. L. Canady, *Scheduling Strategies for Middle Schools*, Larchmont, N.Y.: Eye on Education, 2000.

Rigby, K., "Health Consequences of Bullying and Its Prevention in Schools," in Juvonen and Graham (2001), pp. 310–331.

Riley, R., Mathematics Equals Opportunity, white paper, Washington, D.C.: U.S. Department of Education, October 20, 1997. Online at http://www.ed.gov/pubs/math/mathemat.pdf (as of May 7, 2003).

Roderick, M., *The Path to Dropping Out: Evidence for Intervention*, Westport, Conn.: Auburn House, 1993.

Roeser, R. W., J. S. Eccles, and C. Freedman-Doan, "Academic Functioning and Mental Health in Adolescence: Patterns, Progressions, and Routes from Childhood," *Journal of Adolescent Research*, Vol. 14, 1999, pp. 135–174.

Roeser, R. W., J. S. Eccles, and A. J. Sameroff, "Academic and Emotional Functioning in Early Adolescence: Longitudinal Relations, Patterns, and Prediction by Experience in Middle School," *Developmental Psychopathology*, No. 10, 1998, pp. 321–352.

Rounds, T. S., and S. Y Osaki, *The Social Organization of Classrooms: An Analysis of Sixth- and Seventh-Grade Activity Structures*, San Francisco: Far West Laboratory, EPSSP-82-5, 1982.

Russell, J. F., "Relationships Between the Implementation of Middle-Level Program Concepts and Student Achievement," *Journal of Curriculum and Supervision*, Vol. 12, No. 2, 1997, pp. 152–168.

Rutter, M., B. Maughan, P. Mortimore, J. Ouston, and A. Smith, *Fifteen Thousand Hours: Secondary Schools and Their Effects on Children*, Cambridge, Mass: Harvard University Press, 1979.

Ryan, B. A., G. R. Adams, T. Gullotta, R. P. Weissberg, and R. L. Hampton, eds., *The Family-School Connection Theory, Research, and Practice*, Thousand Oaks: Sage Publications, 1995,

Scales, P. C., and C. K. McEwin, *Growing Pains: The Making of America's Middle School Teachers*, Columbus, Ohio: National Middle School Association, 1994.

Schmidt, W. H., *Mathematics and Science in the Eighth Grade: Findings From the Third International Mathematics and Science Study*, Washington, D.C.: U.S. Department of Education, National Center for Education Statistics, July 2000.

Schmidt, W. H., P. M. Jakwerth, and C. C. McKnight, "Curriculum-Sensitive Assessment: Content Does Make a Difference," *International Journal of Educational Research*, Vol. 29, No. 6, 1998, pp. 503–527.

Schmidt, W., C. McKnight, L. Cogan, P. Jakwerth, and R. Houang, *Facing the Consequences: Using TIMSS for a Closer Look at U.S. Mathematics and Science Education*, Dordrecht, Netherlands: Kluwer, 1999.

Schmidt, W. H., and G. Valverde, Policy Lessons from TIMSS, paper prepared for the National Governors Association, 1997.

Schools and Staffing Survey (SASS), National Center for Education Statistics, U.S. Department of Education, 2001.

Schroth, G., and J. Dixon, "The Effects of Block Scheduling on Student Performance," *International Journal of Educational Reform*, Vol. 5, No. 4, 1996, pp. 472–476.

Schwartz, D., and A. H. Gorman, "Community Violence Exposure and Children's Academic Functioning," *Journal of Educational Psychology*, No. 95, 2003, pp. 163–173.

Shann, M. H., "Academics and a Culture of Caring: The Relationship Between School Achievement and Prosocial and Antisocial Behaviors in Four Urban Middle Schools," *School Effectiveness and School Improvement*, No. 10, 1999, pp. 390–413.

Shepard, L. A., R. Glaser, R. L. Linn, and G. Bohrnstedt, *Setting Performance Standards for Student Achievement: A Report of the National Academy of Education Panel on the Evaluation of the NAEP Trial State Assessment: An Evaluation of the 1992 Achievement Levels,* Stanford, Calif.: Stanford University and the National Academy of Education, 1993.

Simmons, R. G., and D. A. Blyth, *Moving into Adolescence: The Impact of Pubertal Change and School Context,* Hawthorn, N.Y.: Random House, 1987.

Skiba, R., "When is Disproportionality Discrimination? The Overrepresentation of Black Students in School Suspension," in W. Ayers, B. Dohrn, and R. Ayers, eds., *Zero Tolerance,* New York: The Free Press, 2001.

Skiba, R., and R. Peterson, "The Dark Side of Zero Tolerance: Can Punishment Lead to Safe Schools?" *Phi Delta Kappan,* No. 80, 1999, pp. 1–12.

Southern Regional Education Board, *Making Middle Grades Work: Raising the Academic Achievement of All Middle Grades Students,* Atlanta, Ga., 2002. Online at http://www.sreb. org/programs/MiddleGrades/publications/Middle_Grades_Work.pdf (as of October 21, 2003).

Spring, J., *The American School, 1642–1985,* New York: Longman, 1986.

SREB—see Southern Regional Education Board.

Stecher, B. M., and G. W. Bohrnstedt, eds., *Class Size Reduction in California: The 1998–1999 Evaluation Findings,* Sacramento, Calif.: California Department of Education, 2000.

St. George, D. M., and S. B. Thomas, "Perceived Risk of Fighting and Actual Fighting Behavior Among Middle School Students," *Journal of School Health,* No. 67, 1997, pp. 178–181.

Stahler, T., "A Comparative Analysis of Specifically Prepared and Generally Prepared Middle School Preservice Teachers," *Action in Teacher Education,* Vol. 17, No. 3, 1995, pp. 23–32.

Steinberg, L. "Autonomy, Conflict, and Harmony in Family Relationships," in S. Feldman and G. Elliot, eds., *At the Threshold: The Developing Adolescent,* Cambridge, Mass: Harvard University Press, 1990, pp. 255–276.

Steinberg, L., J. Elmen, and N. Mounts, "Authoritative Parenting, Psychosocial Maturity, and Academic Success Among Adolescents," *Child Development,* No. 60, 1989, pp. 1424–1436.

Stevenson, H. W., and J. W. Stigler, *The Learning Gap,* New York: Summit Books, 1992.

Stigler, J. W., and J. Hiebert, *The Teaching Gap: Best Ideas from the World's Teachers for Improving Education in the Classroom,* New York: The Free Press, 1999.

Suter, L. E., "Is Student Achievement Immutable? Evidence from International Studies on Schooling and Student Achievement," *RER,* Vol. 70, No. 4, 2000, pp. 529–545.

Swanson, C. B., and D. L Stevenson, "Standards-Based Reform in Practice: Evidence on State Policy and Classroom Instruction from the NAEP State Assessments," *Educational Evaluation and Policy Analysis*, Vol. 24, No. 1, 2002, pp. 1–27.

Tabachnick, B. G., and L. S. Fidell, *Using Multivariate Statistics*, 3rd ed., New York: Harper & Row, 1989.

Tanner, J. M., *Growth At Adolescence*, 2nd ed., Oxford: Blackwell Scientific Publications, 1962.

Teske, P., and M. Schneider, *The Importance of Leadership: the Role of School Principals*, Arlington, Va.: The Price Waterhouse Coopers Endowment for the Business of Government, 1999.

Thayer, Y. V., and T. L. Shortt, "Block Scheduling Can Enhance School Climate," *Educational Leadership*, Vol. 56, No. 4, 1999, pp. 76–81.

Thorkildsen, R., and M. R. Scott Stein, "Is Parent Involvement Related to Student Achievement? Exploring the Evidence," Phi Delta Kappa Center for Evaluation, Development, and Research, Research Bulletin No. 22, November 11, 1998. Online at http://www.pdkintl.org/edres/resbul22.htm (as of October 21, 2003).

Trimble, S., "What Works to Improve Student Achievement," Westerville, Ohio: National Middle School Association, Research Summary No. 20, 2003. Online at http://www.nmsa.org/research/summary/studentachievement.htm (as of October 21, 2003).

Trusty, Jerry, "Effects of Eighth-Grade Parental Involvement on Late Adolescents' Educational Expectations," *Journal of Research and Development in Education*, Vol. 32, No. 4, 1999, pp. 224–233.

Tyack, D., and L. Cuban, *Tinkering Toward Utopia: A Century of Public School Reform*, Cambridge, Mass.: Harvard University Press, 1995.

United Nations Children's Fund, Innocenti Research Centre, *A League Table of Educational Disadvantage in Rich Nations*, Florence, Italy: UNICEF, Innocenti Report Card No. 4, 2002. Online at: http://www.unicef.org (as of October 21, 2003).

U.S. Census Bureau, About Metropolitan and Micropolitan Statistical Areas, Web site, 2003. Online at http://www.census.gov/population/www/estimates/aboutmetro.htm (as of November 4, 2003).

U.S. Department of Education, National Center for Education Statistics, Common Core of Data 2000–2001.

_____, *Fast Response Survey System, Principal/School Disciplinarian Survey of School Violence*, FRSS 63, 1997.

_____, Office of Elementary and Secondary Education, Academic Improvement and Teacher Quality Programs, *Improving Teacher Quality: Non-Regulatory Guidance*, rev. draft, Washington, D.C., September 12, 2003.

Valentine, J., D. Clark, D. Hackman, and V. Petzko, *A National Study of Leadership in Middle Level Schools: A National Study of Middle Level Leaders and School Programs*, Vol. 1, Reston, Va.: National Association of Secondary School Principals, 2002.

Valentine, J. W., and T. Whitaker, *Organizational Trends and Practices in Middle Level Schools*, in Irvin (1997), pp. 277–283.

Van Til, W., G. Vars, and J. Lounsbury, *Modern Education for the Junior High School Years*, New York: Boobs-Merrill, 1961.

Van Zandt, L. M., and S. Totten, "The Current Status of Middle Level Education Research: A Critical Review," *Research in Middle Level Education*, Vol. 18, No. 3, 1995 pp. 1–25.

Warburton, E. C., R. Bugarin, A. Nunez, and C. D. Carroll, *Bridging the Gap: Academic Preparation and Postsecondary Success of First-Generation Students*, Washington, D.C.: U.S. Government Printing Office, NCES 2001-153, 2001.

Warren, L. L., and K. D. Muth, "The Impact of Common Planning Time on Middle Grade Students and Teachers," *Research in Middle Level Education Quarterly*, Vol. 18, No. 3, 1995, pp. 41–58.

Wehlage, G. G., and R. A. Rutter, *Dropping Out: How Much do Schools Contribute to the Problem?* Madison, Wisc.: Wisconsin Center for Educational Research, University of Wisconsin-Madison, 1985.

Weinstein, R. S., "Overcoming Inequality in Schooling: A Call to Action for Community Psychology," *American Journal of Community Psychology*, Vol. 30, 2002, pp. 21–40.

Wigfield, A., J. S. Eccles, and P. R. Pintrich, "Development Between the Ages of 11 and 25," in D. C. Berliner and R. C. Calfee, eds., *Handbook of Educational Psychology*, New York: Simon & Schuster Macmillan, 1996, pp. 148–185.

Williams, D. L., and N. F. Chavkin, "Essential Elements of Strong Parent Involvement Programs," *Educational Leadership*, Vol. 47, 1989, pp. 18–20.

Williamson, R., and J. H. Johnston, "Challenging Orthodoxy: An Emerging Agenda for Middle Level Reform," *Middle School Journal*, March 1999, pp. 10–17.

Wilson, S. M., R. E. Floden, and J. Ferrini-Mundy, *Teacher Preparation Research: Current Knowledge, Gaps and Recommendations*, Seattle: Center for the Study of Teaching and Policy, University of Washington, 2001.

World Health Organization, *Health Behavior in School Aged Children 1997–1998*, Technical report, Universitetet I Bergen, Research Center for Health Promotion, 1998.

_____, Health Behavior in School Aged Children 1997/1998 Database (U.S. and International).

Young, B., *Common Core Data: Characteristics of the 100 Largest Public Elementary and Secondary School Districts in the United States: 2000-01*, Washington, D.C.: U.S. Government Printing Office, NCES 2002-351, 2002.

Ziegler, S., and L. Mulhall, "Establishing and Evaluating a Successful Advisory Program in a Middle School," *Middle School Journal*, Vol. 25, No. 4, pp. 42–46, 1994.

Zill, N., and J. West, *Entering Kindergarten: Findings from the Condition of Education 2000*, Washington, D.C.: U.S. Government Printing Office, NCES 2001-035, 2001.